CREATIVE
NEEDLECRAFT
HANDBOOK

a practical guide to techniques with over 65
step–by–step projects shown in 1000 photographs

LUCINDA GANDERTON

southwater

For my sister, Emma, with love.

This edition is published by Southwater, an imprint of Anness Publishing Ltd,
Blaby Road, Wigston, Leicestershire LE18 4SE; info@anness.com

www.southwaterbooks.com; www.annesspublishing.com

If you like the images in this book and would like to investigate using them for publishing,
promotions or advertising, please visit our website www.practicalpictures.com for more information.

Publisher: Joanna Lorenz
Senior Editor: Belinda Wilkinson
Designer: Martin Lovelock
Photographer: James Duncan
Step Photographer: Madeleine Brehaut
Stylist: Lucinda Ganderton

Thanks to Anne Cree

© Anness Publishing Ltd 2012

A CIP catalogue record for this book is available from the British Library.

Previously published as *The Needlecraft Book*

MEASUREMENTS
Both imperial and metric measurements have been given in the text. Where conversions produced an
awkward number, these have been rounded for convenience, but will produce an accurate result if one
system is followed throughout.

PUBLISHER'S NOTE
Although the advice and information in this book are believed to be accurate and true at the time
of going to press, neither the authors nor the publisher can accept any legal responsibility or liability
for any errors or omissions that may have been made nor for any inaccuracies nor for any loss,
harm or injury that comes about from following instructions or advice in this book.

Contents

INTRODUCTION	6	CROCHET	190
		Introduction	192
EMBROIDERY	8	Tools and Materials	194
Introduction	10	Techniques	196
Tools and Materials	12	Projects	206
Techniques	14		
Projects	34	SPECIAL TECHNIQUES	
		Dyeing	222
NEEDLEPOINT	58	Fabric-strip Rugs	226
Introduction	60	Smocking	228
Tools and Materials	62	Ribbons and Bows	230
Techniques	64	Tassels and Pompoms	232
Projects	76	Beads and Sequins	234
		Buttons	236
PATCHWORK AND QUILTING	88		
Introduction	90	TEMPLATES	238
Tools and Materials	92		
Techniques	94	ACKNOWLEDGMENTS	252
Projects	108		
		SUPPLIERS	253
APPLIQUÉ	122		
Introduction	124	GLOSSARY	254
Tools and Materials	126	INDEX	255
Techniques	128	CONVERSION TABLES	256
Projects	138		
KNITTING	154		
Introduction	156		
Tools and Materials	158		
Techniques	160		
Projects	174		

Introduction

Traditional needlecrafts form an essential part of our lives and have been carried on throughout the world for centuries in their many forms. In the past, sewing skills were a very necessary part of running a household. Clothing had to be made and patched, socks needed to be darned and domestic linen repaired. It was only the leisured classes who could indulge in the more refined arts of delicate embroidery, white crochet lace or ornate crazy patchwork, as a way of passing the long hours and to show off their skills. For most women needlecrafts were part of the daily routine or a means of earning a living.

Domestic needlework in the early twentieth century was dominated by dressmaking and hand knitting, but society has changed immensely since then. Recent years have seen a major

This multimedia collage uses stitching and colour to bold effect.

revival of interest in all types of decorative and functional needlecraft. There has been a proliferation of craft manuals and magazines, and a plethora of materials is now available from specialist suppliers.

It seems that we are all seeking an escape from the mass produced uniformity of shop-bought products. Even the most basic knowledge of how to sew can enable us to personalize clothing, create original gifts for friends and family, or stitch soft furnishings to make our homes more distinctive and individual.

This book is intended both as a guide to long-established crafts and as an introduction to new and creative ways of working. Its seven chapters in turn cover embroidery, needlepoint, patchwork and quilting, appliqué, knitting and crochet, and there is a

final section which features more specialized ways of working. There are detailed technique sections for each topic, which cover everything from the groundwork of learning knitting and crochet stitches, different ways of piecing patchwork and appliqué, specific embroidery methods such as Assisi work or blackwork, and contemporary crafts such as ribbon-weaving and space dyed yarn.

To put these techniques into practice, there are seventy-five exciting needlecraft projects, designed by leading crafts people, which are aimed

The emotional impact of embroidery is illustrated by this expressive rendering of a woman's face in tent stitch on canvas.

The expert dollmaker who created this striking punk figure constructed the doll's garments from fabric made by the newest machine embroidery techniques.

Needlepoint cushions (pillows) have been popular since the eighteenth century; this modern design is based on the imagery of Indian decoration.

uses. The recent development of materials such as water-soluble fabrics, metallic threads and iron-on fusible bondings mean that ideas can now find even more new and innovative expression.

There is a vast international field of various needlecrafts to draw ideas and inspiration from, and many excellent reference books devoted to topics that are dealt with here in a few pages. *The Complete Guide to Needlecraft* shows how to exploit modern techniques, while remaining true to tradition, and serves as a comprehensive introduction to a wide range of fascinating crafts.

at both the experienced needleworker and the beginner. Some of them are quick to do and can be made in an afternoon; others are more complex and offer a longer term challenge. All the projects are carefully explained with easy to follow step-by-step photographs, and all the necessary templates, charts and patterns are included at the back of the book.

Embroiderers, quiltmakers and knitters have always been inventive. All sewing was done by hand until the arrival of the sewing machine in the l870s. This was welcomed as a relief from the tedium of straight seaming, but its decorative applications were immediately recognized. The swing needle, or zigzag machine has opened up new ways of embroidering which are still being explored. Over the centuries, unusual items such as shells, feathers, ribbons and even hair and iridescent beetle wings have been incorporated with velvets, silks, beads and sequins to create decorative works, and all kinds of yarns and fabrics have been adapted to sometimes unexpected

Contemporary designers are breaking down the boundaries between embroidery and other crafts. This vase of flowers combines the precision of machine stitching with randomly torn coloured paper.

Embroidery

E mbroidery, or the use of decorative stitchery, is an ancient craft which can be reinterpreted in a highly personal style today. The possibilities for combining threads and stitches are endless, and almost any fabric or garment can be embroidered either by hand or machine. This section introduces the basic techniques, and the exciting projects include original accessories for the home and items to wear, to keep or to give as presents.

Embroidery

Embroidery can be defined as the decoration of an existing fabric with ornamental stitches. The art has a long and fascinating history, originating in the opulent colours and stitchery of the Middle East, which arrived in Europe during the time of the Roman Empire. Historically, splendid embroidery was an outward expression of wealth: gold or silver threads, the finest silks, pearls and precious stones have always been used to adorn the robes of kings and emperors and to symbolize their power. Hand-embroidered clothes still have great ceremonial significance: many brides wear gowns encrusted with beads and elaborate stitchery, and whitework christening gowns are treasured heirlooms. Much of the early work that has survived is ecclesiastical. Church embroidery was influenced by the rich ornament of Byzantium and reached its peak in the *Opus Anglicanum*, or English Work, of the thirteenth and fourteenth centuries. A trade network existed via which the London workshops sent vestments to the popes in Rome.

The majority of the secular embroidery work was of a military and heraldic nature, the most famous

A bag of oranges was the inspiration for this machine-embroidered piece, which is worked on paper over a watercolour illustration.

example being the Bayeux Tapestry. It dates from shortly after the invasion of England by William the Conqueror in 1066 and gives a narrative record of the events of that year.

Heraldic banners and flags were used in battle to identify groups of soldiers and are still carried ceremonially by the armed forces. Alongside the military versions, the old craft guilds and later, trade unions, developed pictorial banners, embroidered with their coats of arms. Members would march behind these as a symbol of solidarity.

Domestic embroidery flowered in the sixteenth century. Contemporary aristocratic portraits show elaborate dresses, often decorated with

blackwork. This was the period when embroidery ceased to be the sole preserve of the nobility, as it spread throughout Europe to the rising merchant classes.

Indigenous embroidery developed strong national characteristics. Different cultures specialized in different techniques, utilizing locally available materials. Exquisite floral Chinese embroidery used fine silk threads, while Native Americans incorporated stained porcupine quills and glass beads in their richly decorative work.

Patterns and techniques, however, have always travelled and developed. Geometric cross stitch, the most widely

Right: This antique embroidered slipper – which was never made up – is worked on a black felt background in laid gold thread and silk floss.

Left: Cross stitch samplers were a learning exercise for the children who made them. Stylized birds, flowers and trees were worked alongside alphabets and improving mottoes.

In the nineteenth century the passion for interior decoration reached great heights. Wealth generated by developing industries meant that more and more people were moving into new homes and wanted to make them unique. By the 1870s most middle-class interiors were decorated with an astonishing array of embroidered piano covers, fire screens, pincushions, candle shades and bell pulls. The Art Needlework movement sought to encourage embroiderers to express themselves by experimenting with new materials and their ingenuity encompassed sewing with ribbons and bows, and on to painted silk.

Taste in the early twentieth century moved away from the excesses of the preceding years and towards a more refined style. Art Nouveau and Art Deco styles were both interpreted in embroidery, but the scope for new design and reworking of tradition has never been greater than it is today.

spread folk art technique in Europe, was taken to the New World by Pennsylvania Dutch immigrants. Settlers took with them their individual textile traditions, but life in America was different and hard, with cloth and thread in short supply. Needlework schools existed in New England from the early eighteenth century, and imported materials and fabrics were more generally available there than on the frontier but, even so, yarn was expensive. Tutors tended, therefore, to instruct embroiderers to outline designs, not to fill them in and, above all, to be economical with the precious thread.

Right: Embroidery has always been used in conjunction with other needlecrafts: strong, simple stitches emphasize the shapes of this contemporary folk-art style appliqué.

11

Embroidery
Tools and Materials

An inspiring selection of fabrics and threads is available which, with imagination, can be combined to produce individual and exciting embroideries. The basic equipment needed is minimal: every sewing box should contain the tools listed, along with pins and sewing thread. A steam iron is necessary for all needlecrafts, to finish work professionally.

From top to bottom, three types of even-weave linen, and one non even-weave linen.

THREADS
Threads come in a broad spectrum of colours. Silk and metallic threads give texture, but the most popular threads are 6-stranded cottons which can be separated for fine stitching. Perlé cotton is a single thread with a shiny finish. Wool threads, including finely spun crewel yarn and 3-stranded Persian yarn, are used singly for embroidery. Machine threads can be glossy or metallic, and some are even space-dyed with stripes.

FABRIC
Ordinary linens are used for free stitchery but single-thread even-weave linens have a regular mesh so that the stitches are even. They are designed for counted thread and pulled or drawn work. There are several types of double-thread even-weaves. The finest is Hardanger fabric which has a count of 22, i.e., there are 22 threads to 2.5cm (1in). 14-count Aida cloth is suitable for cross stitch and 6-count Binca is ideal for beginners. Narrow bands of fabric with woven edges are also available.

From left to right, woven Aida bands with decorative edging in blue and red, and natural linen.

FRAMES
Adjustable tapestry or scroll frames are best for large pieces, while hoops suit most other work. They can be bought with stands so that the user's hands are left free to work the piece. Round plastic frames with metal inner rings are especially good for machine embroidery.

TOOLS AND ACCESSORIES
Needles come in different widths and lengths, the most useful being large-eyed crewel needles. Tapestry needles are thick and blunt, while chenille needles are larger but pointed.

Long-bladed dressmaker's shears are essential for cutting fabric and a small pair of sharp embroidery scissors is needed for threads. An unpicker is always very useful for correcting mistakes and a thimble protects the finger.

Water-soluble or fading dressmaker's felt-tip pens are used to mark directly on to fabric. Carbon pencils and dressmaker's carbon will transfer designs from paper to cloth.

From top to bottom, Hardanger fabric, Aida cloth in white and green, Binca.

Perlé cotton.

Metallic thread.

Machine embroidery threads.

Silk threads.

Needles.

Dressmaker's pins.

Dressmaker's shears.

Embroidery scissors.

Thimble.

Crewel yarn.

Unpicker.

Six-strand
cotton or
embroidery
floss.

Dressmaker's fading pen.

Transfer pencil.

Dressmaker's carbon.

Persian yarn.

Wooden hoop or round frame.

Plastic hoops.

Tapestry or scroll frame.

Starting Off

Most embroidery should be worked in a frame to allow an even stitch tension and to prevent the fabric becoming distorted. A tapestry frame is suitable for larger pieces of work but for small hand-stitched projects and all machine embroidery, a two-part hoop frame is used. To keep delicate fabrics taut, the inner ring can be bound with bias binding.

Right: Hoop frames are easy to manage and portable, and can be used for working larger pieces by changing the position when each area is completed, although this may cause distortion to finer embroidery.

1 USING A FRAME
To mount the cloth in the hoop, loosen the screw on the outer ring and separate the two parts. Place the fabric over the inner ring and press the outer ring down in place.

2 Stretch the fabric so that it is taut. Be sure that the weave lies squarely as shown. Tighten the screw. For machine embroidery the fabric should be right side up with the stitching area at the bottom of the hoop.

1 BEGINNING TO STITCH Working threads should not be longer than 45cm (18in) or they will fray and become tangled. The needle selected should always be the right size for the thread and fabric; a small eye can harm the thread, while a thick needle will leave large holes. Threads have a natural tendency to twist back on themselves; if this happens, let the needle and thread hang down and untwist. It is not advisable to anchor the thread with a knot at the back as it may distort the surface. Instead, when starting the first stitches of a piece, make a knot and insert the needle from the front, a short distance away from the area to be worked, so that the thread will be held fast at the back by the stitching. The knot can then be snipped off.

2 Subsequent threads can be started off by slipping the needle under the back of the existing stitches and working a back stitch. Finish off in the same way, and trim the loose ends.

Transferring and Charting

P atterns can be transferred on to a background in several ways; the choice depends on the nature of the design itself as well as the fabric and thread to be used. It is important that any lines marked should not show through the stitches; dressmaker's pens are now available which are either water-soluble or which fade completely over time. These are particularly suitable for fine freehand drawing or tracing directly on to the fabric via a light box. A chalk pencil can be used for bolder designs. Dressmaker's carbon paper is also used for indirect tracing and is best for smooth fabrics.

Right: The strawberry motif makes a perfect decoration for this ready-made lacy jam-pot cover.

1 TISSUE TACKING (BASTING) This is used for textured materials such as velvet, where a drawn line would not show. Trace the design on to tissue paper then pin to the right side of the fabric. With a contrasting thread, work over the design using a small running stitch.

2 When complete, carefully tear away the tissue paper without pulling the thread. The embroidery is then worked over this guideline and any tacking (basting) which remains can be cut away.

TRANSFER PENCIL Using an embroidery transfer pencil and thin paper, trace the design. If the pattern is symmetrical or needs to be reversed, place the paper, with the pencil side down, on to the fabric, pin in place and press with a cool iron. For an outline which is the same as the original, trace it with a pencil, turn the paper and draw over the lines with the transfer pencil.

CROSS STITCH CHARTS The regular format of cross stitch makes it ideal for charting designs on to graph paper, where one square represents one stitch. Trace the design on to special tracing paper printed with a grid, as shown, or transfer it on to squared paper. Fill in the outline with coloured pens or pencils, to match the colours to be used.

Straight Stitches

There is an enormous variety of traditional stitches which provide the foundation for hand embroidery and sewing throughout the world. Some may be intricately textured or interwoven with precious gold thread; others use a simple row of stranded cotton to outline a design, or form twisted knots to make a single point of colour. All of them, however, are derived from three basic ways of working: straight, looped or knotted stitches. A wide range of textures and effects can be achieved just by using simple variations of flat, straight stitches. They can be worked in rows, at different angles and in varying sizes or combined to produce geometric shapes.

Right: These satin stitch butterflies were stitched with shiny silk thread on this piece of antique Chinese embroidery.

RUNNING STITCH This is the most basic of stitches, and is used to join pieces of fabric, outline motifs and for quilting. The stitches should all be equal in length and evenly spaced. A long running stitch is used for tacking (basting).

WHIP STITCH A contrasting thread is woven through a basic line of running stitch to give a twisted effect to this stitch. Be careful not to pick up any of the background fabric.

BACK STITCH This consists of a continuous line of even stitches. The needle is carried behind the work for twice the length of the finished stitch. It is used for outlines, especially in Assisi or blackwork.

STEM STITCH Also known as crewel stitch, this is similar to back stitch. The thread should always lie to one side of the needle. The width can be altered by varying the stitch angle.

SEED STITCH Short detached stitches, all measuring the same length, are worked at random to produce a powdered filling, or to add pattern to a plain area. As a variation, two parallel stitches can be worked to give a more raised surface.

SATIN STITCH It may take some practice to achieve the distinctive smooth finish and tidy edge of this versatile stitch. The individual stitches, which should not be too long, are all worked in the same direction.

The main shape of this "naive" fish is outlined in back stitch, with an irregular running stitch infill. Its strong graphic impact comes from the use of white thread on a dark fabric.

ARROWHEAD STITCH Two equal straight stitches at right angles form the arrow points, which can be evenly spaced in regular rows or worked as random individual stitches to give a scattered filling over a larger area.

CHEVRON STITCH This looks particularly effective when worked on striped or spotted fabric. It is made up of a line of straight stitches worked at right angles to each other with a short back stitch at the intersection point.

FERN STITCH This gives a leafy effect, which is ideal for plant designs. It is made up of three small stitches radiating from a point, and can be worked in straight or curved lines, or detached as a filling stitch.

This Indian bird is worked entirely in straight stitches and uses coloured cottons on a natural linen background. It is framed by a triple row of interlaced running stitch.

Cross Stitches

A basic cross stitch is formed by working one straight stitch across another. There are several variations where the angle of the cross is altered or the stitches overlap, and all can be worked in rows or singly. The regular pattern produced by all these stitches is ideally suited for embroidering on ginghams, striped fabrics or even-weave linen. Cross stitch is the foundation for the traditional embroidery of many cultures, from ancient Egyptian textiles to the geometric designs of modern Scandinavian work.

In the past, children learnt to sew by practising cross stitch samplers, and today a wide range of charted designs is available.

Narrow strips of even-weave fabric with decorative borders can be bought by length and are ideal for making small gift items such as bookmarks, decorative cake-ribbons or these monogrammed napkin rings.

CROSS STITCH This stitch can be worked individually for outlines and letters, but is usually made in two separate rows, as shown, when a larger area has to be covered. The second line of stitches should always lie in the same direction for an even appearance.

HERRINGBONE STITCH This is often used to form a border around work and is particularly effective when stitched between two lines on a striped fabric. It is worked from left to right with an even space between the overlapping arms.

LACED HERRINGBONE STITCH Extra interest can be added to plain herringbone stitch by interlacing it with a contrasting colour. A blunt needle is used to prevent any of the foundation fabric getting caught up, and the thread should not be pulled too tightly.

CLOSED HERRINGBONE STITCH This is worked as for herringbone but the space between the stitches is closed up. It is sometimes sewn on the reverse of a fine fabric so that the front gives the appearance of two lines of back stitch and the diagonal stitches are visible through the cloth. This technique is known as "shadow work".

DOUBLE HERRINGBONE STITCH To produce an interlaced effect, the needle is passed down and below the upward stitches on the first row, so that they all lie above the downward stitches. The second row uses a contrasting colour, and is worked in the same way, with the upward stitches threaded under the downward stitches of the first row.

LONGARM CROSS STITCH This overlapping stitch produces a dense, braided finish and is useful for heavy outlines. It is worked from left to right, with a longer and more slanted second arm and the diagonals meet at the top and bottom.

DOUBLE CROSS STITCH This star-shaped stitch can be worked individually or in lines. It is made up of two simple cross stitches worked one over the other.

ERMINE FILLING An upright straight stitch is overlapped with a single cross stitch to produce a six-pointed star, which can be repeated at random or in regular rows for a more formal effect.

Left: The cross stitch samplers of the nineteenth century were embroidered with alphabets, mottoes and pictorial motifs. This typical carnation border is a combination of both geometric and floral elements.

Right: This lavender sachet is made from Aida cloth, a woven fabric which is produced especially for cross stitch work. It is easy to use, as there is no need for complicated thread counting, and is available in a range of sizes and colours.

Assisi Work

This historic variation originated in the Italian town of Assisi. It reverses the usual method of working cross stitch patterns – with striking results. The main motifs are first outlined with a single line and the background filled in with solid rows of cross stitch. The stylized imagery is based on birds, fish and animals – both real and mythical – along with geometric and floral motifs. It underwent a revival in the early 1900s, when the old patterns were redrawn. It is traditionally worked on cream or white evenweave linen, using a combination of red, blue and black embroidery threads.

Right: This heraldic dragon is worked in black against red and edged with a Greek key pattern. Single stitches emphasize the claws and the eye is marked with a detached cross stitch.

1 Work the motif and border with Holbein stitch, which resembles back stitch. This is sewn as two rounds of running stitch, the second row filling the spaces left between the first.

2 The background is completely filled with cross stitch, in a bright primary colour. The stitches can be worked singly, or, as is usual with this technique, back and forth in rows.

3 The elaborate linear border is worked in Holbein stitch, using the main colour again.

On a much smaller scale, these two ducks (above) were adapted from a pattern card, published in the early twentieth century when there was a great renewal of interest in Assisi work.

Blackwork

Blackwork uses straight and back stitches to create small-scale all-over patterns. This distinctive embroidery became popular in sixteenth-century England, when it was used to decorate caps, gloves, sleeves and bodices. Design at that time was naturalistic; the geometric repeats of blackwork were worked to fill in the flowing outlines of flower petals, leaves and fruit. It is traditionally done using stranded cotton on even-weave linen, but Aida cloth provides a quicker alternative.

Right: Different patterns all have their own tonal value, ranging from dark to light, depending on how the stitches are arranged. This sampler features some old and new variations (clockwise from top right): *Algerian eye stitch* consists of eight straight stitches radiating from a central point; *Zigzag stitch* is worked in diagonal rows of stepped back stitch; *Fishscale stitch* is built up in rows of short straight stitches, linked with a zigzag; *Shoofly stitch* consists of four triangles arranged at the points of a cross stitch; *Grid stitch* consists of separate motifs, which may be joined with diagonal back stitches; *Pinwheel stitch* is worked in back stitch as a series of individual shapes; *Square stitch*, a half-drop repeat, can be made singly or by working rows of running stitch; and *Lattice stitch* is a deceptively simple pattern of interlocking diamonds and squares.

There is an infinite array of geometric patterns that can be used for blackwork (above). Any tiny shape can be adapted by charting it on to graph paper and working out a repeat. The border of a fragment of broken pottery was the inspiration for this series of single motifs and all-over fillings.

The symmetry of blackwork means that the most basic computer graphics package can be used to produce suitable patterns. This computer-designed example (left) has the appearance of a piece of very traditional work, but is, in fact, a marriage of old and new.

21

Looped and Knotted Stitches

Instead of simply sewing in and out of the background as for the previous stitches, the stitches in this group are all formed by looping the thread and holding it down on the surface, either with further stitches, or by passing the needle through the thread to form a knot. Variations range from functional blanket stitch to the raised textures of bullion and French knots. Chain and feather stitches can be worked quickly and produce a decorative effect, which is popular for "crazy" patchwork. It is important that all of these stitches are worked with an even tension and that the loops are not pulled tightly.

Above: This Indian marriage cloth is embroidered with a variety of stitches, which includes rows of closely worked chain stitch to define squares and chevrons.

CHAIN STITCHES

Chain stitch
Pass the needle down and under the fabric for the correct length and pull through, keeping the thread tucked below the point. Work the next stitch through the loop, into the hole where the thread emerged.

Threaded chain stitch A row of evenly spaced detached chain stitches forms the foundation for this double link chain. Each one is secured below the loop with a small stitch. A contrasting thread is threaded under the loops in each direction.

Lazy daisy stitch Single chain stitches are sewn in the round to form this popular flower shape. Each flower should be arranged evenly in a circle and worked from the centre out. Further single stitches can be used to make leaves.

Blanket stitch This can be worked as an edging or surface stitch, or closely together for buttonholes. It is worked from left to right, in a row of regular upright stitches, with the thread always passing under the needle.

Feather stitch This is worked from top to bottom as a series of alternate slanting stitches. Again, the thread always lies under the needle to form the characteristic loops. It is often used in conjunction with smocking.

Double feather stitch This border stitch is an elaboration of the basic feather stitch. Two stitches, instead of one, are made to one side and then to the other. It can be varied by changing the angle.

KNOTTED STITCHES *French knot* Bring the needle out and hold the thread taut. Wrap it twice round the needle and tighten the thread. Push the needle back through the fabric, close to the point from which it emerged.

Bullion knot The method is similar to the French knot. Start off with a back stitch of the required length. Wrap the thread round several times and hold it down as the needle is pulled carefully through the loops and inserted back at the start.

Coral stitch This attractive outline can be worked regularly or so that the knots are spaced at random. Pass the needle through a small amount of fabric at an angle, looping the thread over the needle and pulling through to form a knot.

Whitework

1 With a dressmaker's pen or soft pencil, draw round the leaf on to the background fabric.

W hitework is a generic term for the many types of white-on-white embroidery, unlike blackwork which describes a single, specialized technique. It is most often used on household linens: tray or tablecloths, pillow covers, nightdress cases, lingerie and handkerchiefs. Variations include the delicate floral Scottish Ayrshire Work, the traditional decoration for christening gowns, Norwegian Hardanger stitchery and the open lace work of *broderie anglaise* (eyelet lace). Mountmellick work is the Irish version of whitework, named after the town in which it was first developed. It is worked in a variety of raised and textured stitches, using a matt (non-shiny) crochet-type thread on a cotton drill (twill) background. Like much other whitework, it draws on the natural imagery of plants, fruit and flowers, but interprets it in a bold, graphic style. It was used to make articles that varied in scale from babies' bibs and collars to bedspreads. Special pattern books and transfers were also produced. A contemporary and personal interpretation is to collect interestingly shaped leaves – from the garden or from a country walk – to use as templates.

This *broderie anglaise* (eyelet lace) sprig was worked by outlining the petals with a narrow satin stitch, then cutting away the surplus fabric to form the distinctive eyelets.

2 Thread a large-eyed needle with crochet cotton and work the veins in stem or back stitch.

Right: A delicate handkerchief was once an essential accessory; this lace-edged antique example is densely embroidered with the owner's initials and a deep border. It is stitched in cotton on a fine lawn ground.

3 Work a closely stitched border of satin or blanket stitch around the outline, and pick out the stalk in stem stitch.

Pulled and Drawn Thread Work

These two techniques are used to create delicate lace-like effects on fine, even-weave fabrics. They have long been classified as whitework, but they can look very dramatic if done in coloured threads or on a patterned fabric. In pulled work the stitches are worked tightly so that the threads of the fabric are forced apart to create a pattern, whereas in drawn thread work threads are removed from the foundation fabric for a more open look.

Right: Interesting areas of texture can be produced by experimenting with the many pulled thread stitches, as in this abstract sampler.

1 PULLED THREAD STITCHES *Algerian eye stitch* This open eyelet is formed by working 16 straight stitches, radiating from a central point. It can be worked singly or in rows.

2 *Honeycomb darning* This regular open background stitch is worked over three threads, in rows from right to left, then left to right.

3 *Single faggot stitch* This filling stitch is worked in stepped diagonal rows, which build up to form a grid.

Above: Beautiful all-over patterns can be produced by working in white thread on white linen. The intricacy of this design is emphasized by a backing of hand-dyed silk.

1 DRAWN THREAD STITCHES *Ladder stitch* These simple examples are worked on loosely woven checked linen, from which bands of thread were removed. Back stitch is used to pull the remaining threads into clusters.

2 *Corded clusters* Solid clusters are made by binding the embroidery thread tightly around groups of foundation threads.

Couching and Laid Thread Work

Couching and laid thread work are two closely related techniques which have been used for centuries when embroidering with textured, silk floss and metallic threads, or narrow cords and ribbons that cannot be drawn through the background fabric. Instead, these threads are attached to the surface with tiny straight or ornamental stitches worked in a finer thread. Couching is a fast and effective way to define curves, outlines and decorative spirals, while laid thread work is generally used to fill motifs and to cover backgrounds. An embroidery frame should always be used for these techniques, to prevent the stitches from puckering. Neither thread should be pulled too tightly or the shapes will distort.

Above: The motifs of this panel are worked in several filling stitches, and show the depth and texture that can be created.

COUCHING *Plain couching* Place the thread to be couched in the position required on the fabric. Make small detached stitches at regular intervals to anchor it down, in a contrasting thread. Tidy the piece by drawing the loose ends to the back of the fabric.

Decorative couching Embroidery stitches such as cross stitch or blanket stitch can be used to secure the laid thread for a more decorative effect. Here square chain stitch is worked through the fabric, across several strands of cotton.

Double couching Two parallel lines of broad metallic thread are held down by a row of feather stitch, with half of the feather stitch being worked over each line of metallic thread.

Spiral couching To fill a circle, bring both threads up in the centre of the circle. Coil the thread to be couched in a spiral, and couch down with the other thread at regular intervals to form a spoked pattern.

1 LAID WORK *Lattice work* Large areas or individual shapes can be covered with this filling stitch. The basic lattice is made by working rows of long parallel stitches, both horizontally and vertically, to form a regular grid.

2 Small contrasting stitches are worked over each thread intersection to secure the long threads to the background and to decorate the grid. Further patterning can be added by working extra stitches within the squares.

Left: This jewel-like patchwork has been assembled from fragments of antique gold and mirror work from northern India. A variety of couching techniques has been used to create the geometric patterns.

Right: Contrasting couched threads have been used to emphasize the outline of these simple animal figures, and to disguise the edges of the appliquéd shapes.

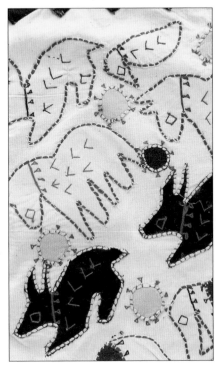

Above: These luxurious and innovative samples use a range of couched techniques, including a spiral of silver wire which is held in place with almost invisible stitches.

Machine Embroidery

Machine embroidery is innovative, quick to work and growing in popularity. Sewing machines have always been used to produce decorative effects, as well as for plain stitching, but the swing-needle machine has great potential as a creative tool. The latest generation of electronic machines is increasingly sophisticated and comes complete with pre-programmed patterns, alphabets and even the capability of scanning in designs. Despite this, exciting effects can still be achieved with the simple straight and zigzag stitches of the standard domestic machine. The instruction manual will have details of any special embroidery feet or attachments which have been supplied and it should be consulted for information about basic stitching methods. Starting to work in this unfamiliar way may seem a little daunting at first, so take time to become familiar with how the machine works and don't be afraid to experiment. Always stitch at the slowest speed and do not race the machine.

FREE STITCHING
For normal use the machine stitch is controlled by the "feed dog" which produces an even stitch by regulating the pace at which the fabric goes under the presser foot. If this is lowered or covered (depending on the machine model – check the manual for details of how to do this) the stitch can be controlled by moving the fabric in the desired direction.

The background and main blocks of plain colour in these amusing illustrations have been filled in with multi-directional satin stitch in varying widths, with the fine details worked in straight stitch.

SATIN STITCH The fabric should be kept taut in a frame, and held lightly with both hands. Thread the machine as normal and set the controls to zigzag. Apply gentle pressure to the pedal and move the frame slowly forwards so that a close satin stitch is built up. The width can be varied by adjusting the controls.

1 STRAIGHT STITCH Lines of straight stitch can be worked in exactly the same way as satin stitch, and if they are made in different directions, interesting textures can be created. The frame can be moved from side to side or back and forth.

2 With practice and experiment, curved and wavy lines can be easily achieved. These are best sewn at a gentle speed so that the background can be manipulated below the presser foot.

Machine embroidery need not be limited to the usual fabrics; the baroque picture frames which surround these batik figures are made from dyed heavyweight interfacing.

Layers of straight stitch can be built up to create a great depth of colour and interest within a piece of work, as in these dynamic portraits of African women.

Once the basic methods have been mastered, machine embroidery can become a very flexible way of "drawing"; this notebook contains a series of experimental images which include more advanced techniques such as changing the tension of either the top or bobbin threads to produce irregular, looped stitches.

29

Working on a Painted Background

Machine embroidery can be used to produce a free outline, which is as flexible as a hand-drawn line. Straight stitch is particularly useful for adding detail to and defining a design, which may be painted on material with fabric paints or with watercolours, gouache or acrylics on to paper.

Right: The colours and shapes of a pineapple inspired this lively tropical design. The yellow stars are given an added dynamism by the diamond shapes that surround them.

1 Choose a design which has clear areas of colour and a strong outline and paint it on to heavy paper; watercolour paper is ideal. Mount the design onto a second, slightly larger, piece of paper for extra support.

2 Thread the machine with black cotton and stitch slowly around the outlines. These can be emphasized by working twice over some areas.

3 Fill in various blocks of colour with a free zigzag stitch, using a thread that is a shade darker than the painted background to give a feeling of depth.

Left: This linen placemat was made in the 1950s, at the time when machine embroidery was first being explored as an art form. It is worked in straight stitch on a screen-printed background.

Working with Paper

Paper can be used like fabric as a background for machine embroidery, but it can also be put to many other uses. It can be painted, torn or cut into shapes and interwoven with ribbons to create interesting multi-layered and collage effects. Be sure that the stitch tension is not too tight when working on paper as it can easily tear.

Above: For this colourful example, bright lines of straight stitch have been sewn to run parallel with the weave. These contrast with the floral motifs sewn on to the surface.

Above: This illustration was made by gluing torn paper shapes on to a plain background, then "drawing" on the black lines in free straight stitch.

1 WOVEN PAPER WITH RIBBONS
Find some gift ribbons and paint cartridge paper with bands of colour to match. Cut into narrow strips and arrange horizontally with the ribbons on the backing paper. Fix with masking tape along one side and interweave the vertical pieces.

2 When the work is the desired size, tape the edges to hold the paper and ribbons in place for stitching.

3 Stitch through the backing, the woven strips and ribbon around the outer edge, then free stitch over the surface in a variety of colours.

Machine Lace

Machine lace fabrics are constructed by building up a network of interlocking stitches on a specially produced background material, which is then removed to leave an open web of thread. This is done by applying heat or by dissolving it in water. There are three different fabrics available, each with special qualities. The working method is the same for all three, however: the rows of stitching must always intersect and cross each other so that the finished piece retains its shape. For extra flexibility in stitching, the presser foot can be taken off. This means that the fabric can be moved in a freer way. It is worth taking time to become familiar with this way of working, by practising on a frame stretched with fine cotton. The hoop must always be held at the outer rim to avoid accidents.

Above: The fins and tail of this exotic fish are worked in a mesh of metallic threads and the glittering body is formed from tiny scraps of shiny fabric and glitter which have been trapped between two layers of bronze organza (organdy).

1 MULTILAYERED WATER-SOLUBLE METHOD Stretch the fabric tautly in a hoop and trace the outline with a felt-tip pen. Use a size 9 needle and thread the machine with metallic machine embroidery thread. Drop or cover the feed dog, set the stitch length to zero, then sew over and within the shape to form a tracery of thread. To create extra colour, add small cuttings of thread and net between two pieces of organza (organdy) and stitch over.

2 Rinse the finished piece in a bowl of water or directly under the cold tap. The backing fabric will simply disappear and all traces can be washed away.

3 Blot the work between layers of paper towel and ease into shape. Leave to dry away from any direct heat.

4 An extra dimension can be added by stiffening the piece with spray varnish. It can then be moulded or shaped and left to dry.

VANISHING MUSLIN is a stiffened loose-weave material which is worked in a frame then pressed under a cloth with a hot iron or put in a pre-warmed oven at 300°F/150°C for five minutes. The heat causes the fibres to discolour and disintegrate.

COLD-WATER-SOLUBLE FABRIC is made from a natural fibre which is a derivative of seaweed. It is delicate and must be worked in a hoop. It is not suitable for very dense sewing – although a double layer can be used if stitching closely – but it is ideal for creating fine multilayered textures, incorporating fragments of decorative cloth and fibre.

HOT-WATER-SOLUBLE FABRIC is stronger and stiffer than the cold-water version. It is used for heavier stitching and can be worked without a frame. The finished piece is then boiled for five minutes in a saucepan of water to dissolve the backing, and then stretched back into shape as it dries.

Below: These dramatic large-scale figures each measure 45cm (18in) high. The embroidery has been worked directly over the wire frames which support them, on a backing of water-soluble fabric, to create a wide range of intricate patterns and textures.

Above: Tiny pearls and fine lace have been used to decorate the golden machine lace garments worn by this ethereal fairy.

Right: The jewel-like effect of metallic machine lace makes it particularly suitable for use in small projects such as earrings. Special jewellery findings are available from most craft stores.

Alphabet Sampler

In the 1800s, schoolteachers and private governesses would combine the teaching of literacy and needlecraft by giving their pupils – both boys and girls – the painstaking task of embroidering a cross stitch sampler. Surviving antique examples, by children as young as six, sometimes exhibit remarkably accomplished sewing skills. Specially printed pattern books were used as a guide and this lower-case alphabet first appeared in a French publication at the turn of the nineteenth century.

MATERIALS

25cm (10in) square of 14-count white Aida cloth
Stranded embroidery threads in burgundy, scarlet, burnt orange, yellow gold and olive green
Embroidery scissors
20cm (8in) square wooden picture frame with glass
Fabric marker pen

1 The layout of the alphabet used here is for a 15cm (6in) square, but it could easily be adapted to fit a rectangular shape. Allowing a 5cm (2in) margin, work the first A in the top left corner, using three strands of burgundy thread. Be sure that all the cross stitches lie in the same direction. Finish off the first colour and, with scarlet thread, work the B. Use burnt orange, yellow gold, then olive green for the next letters and continue working the alphabet, keeping the same sequence of colours in each row.

2 Press the finished embroidery lightly from the back. Place the glass from the frame on to the right side and centre the design. Cut a piece of card to fit the frame, fold the edges of the fabric around the card and lace tightly at the back.

Potpourri Bag

Simple checked fabric has long been produced in many parts of the world and is a favourite choice for household textiles. This homespun cotton potpourri bag is inspired by the functional hand-woven cloth made by the American Shaker community. Its square weave forms a good basis for the counted threads of cross stitch and the contrasting heart motif fits neatly into the blue and white squared pattern. The natural texture of the raffia tie gives the finished bag a country-style appeal.

MATERIALS

23 x 33cm (9 x 13in) piece of checked fabric
Stranded embroidery thread in dark pink
Matching cotton sewing thread
Dressmaker's pins
Potpourri, lavender flowers or sweet-scented dried herbs
Length of garden raffia

1 Following the chart given, embroider three cross stitch hearts, spaced evenly along one half of one long edge of the fabric. Use three strands of the thread and work over three or four threads of fabric, depending on the size of the weave. Make sure that the stitches are all worked in the same direction.

2 Fold the short edges together, with the embroidery on the inside. Pin together the short edges, and the bottom (with embroidery). Hand or machine stitch, leaving a 12mm (½in) seam allowance. Fold the open top edge over and hem on the wrong side.

3 Clip the corners, then turn the bag right side out and press lightly. Fill the bag with potpourri, lavender flowers or sweet-scented dried herbs. Tie a length of raffia around the top of the bag to make a decorative bow. Make a hanging loop from another, shorter length of raffia.

Cross Stitch Motifs

Counted cross stitch motifs are quick to work, easy to adapt and can be mounted in a variety of ways to make personalized presents for all occasions. Specialist manufacturers produce an interesting range of items designed to display lace or small pieces of embroidery. These include boxes, powder bowls (jars), Christmas-tree decorations, jewellery and glass paperweights. Greetings-card blanks are available in assorted shapes and sizes, including ones small enough to make gift tags.

Right: All the designs in this project are worked with three strands of embroidery thread on 12- or 14-count Aida cloth, which is woven specially for cross stitch work. It is more convenient to use than evenweave linen, as the individual threads of cloth do not have to be counted. Each symbol on the chart in the template section at the end of the book represents one cross-stitch.

1 By experimenting with different-coloured embroidery threads and background fabrics, strikingly varied interpretations of a single motif can be created. Aida cloth is available in a range of colours and can also be dyed using cold-water dyes. This design can be worked in dark green with two shades of pink as a romantic rose garland; in pale pink and light green to look like a wreath of apples; or in toning orange colours for a warm country feel.

2 The rose garland makes a perfect dressing-table ornament, when displayed on the lid of a crystal powder bowl (jar). Follow the supplier's instructions for assembling the various components and ensure that the motif lies centrally by lining it up with the lid before cutting it out.

3 The antique feel of the cast pewter frame complements the soft colours of the apple wreath, while the smooth gold adds extra warmth to the bright orange variation.

THE SCANDINAVIAN HEART is an ideal design for a Christmas card and could be worked as a single motif or repeated to create an all-over design.

TO MAKE A VALENTINE HEART CARD Some card blanks are produced with an adhesive area for mounting embroidery, but double-sided sticky tape is a good alternative for mounting work. Check that the design is aligned correctly in the space before gluing down the back of the cardboard.

Left: TO MAKE THE WOVEN HEART Work all the white areas first, before the red. Green fabric emphasizes the colour contrast, but a softer choice of threads would transform the design into a valentine heart.

THE WOVEN HEART The festive combination of red and white is a favourite choice in Norway, the source of this woven heart pattern.

Right: THE LITTLE SCHOOLHOUSE design is adapted from an American quilting block. It would make an apt gift to welcome somebody to their new home.

Fabric Book

This fabric-covered book could be put to many uses: as a photo album containing pictures of a special event, as a sketchbook or as a notebook in which to write down favourite quotations and memories. The direct naive style of the birds and the tree is reminiscent of the Pennsylvania Dutch folk tradition, but the interpretation is fresh and contemporary.

Cotton fabrics with small-scale floral designs, sometimes known as "charm" prints and sold specifically for making patchwork, are best suited to this project.

MATERIALS

2 pieces of mounting board 23 x 28cm (9 x 11in)
Masking tape
2 sheets of watercolour paper
56 x 33cm (22 x 13in) piece of floral fabric
Strong (heavy-duty) white thread
Double-sided sticky tape
28 x 75cm (11 x 30in) piece of gingham
Pinking shears
Stranded embroidery thread in yellow, dark green, dark pink, light pink, brown, light green, blue and violet;
Small pieces of hessian (burlap)
Iron-on fusible bonding;
2 other floral fabrics
Small red and blue glass beads
Gold lurex thread
25cm (10in) length of narrow ribbon

1 Join the two pieces of mounting board along both sides of one long edge with masking tape. Check they can close easily. Cut the water-colour paper to size for the inside pages, fold in half and sew into the spine with strong (heavy-duty) thread. Cover the outside of the book with floral fabric, securing with double-sided tape. Line the inside with gingham. Cut a square of gingham to fit on to the front cover, pink the edges and embroider the border with yellow cross stitch. Stick on to the front of the book with double-sided tape.

2 Cut the hessian (burlap) to fit inside the gingham and fray the edge. Enlarging as necessary, trace the tree, hill and bird from the template on to separate pieces of fusible bonding. Iron on to the back of the floral fabrics and cut out; cut two birds. Remove the backing paper and iron the hill and tree on to the hessian (burlap).

3 Secure the hill and tree with small, dark green stitches. Embroider the leaves in light green by making four small back-stitches and winding the thread around them, or making detached chain stitches. Work lines of brown chain-stitch along the tree trunk and branches.

4 Iron the birds into position. Sew on blue beads for the eyes and stitch the wings in pink, as for leaves. The tail is worked with three detached chain stitches in yellow and blue.

5 Embroider each flower by making a French knot in yellow and surrounding it with five detached chain stitches in blue or violet. Make a stem with a straight stitch in light green and work a leaf. Couch three stars in the sky with gold lurex and sew a few red beads on to the tree as berries.

6 Finish off by working blanket stitch in light pink around the edge of the hessian (burlap) and sticking it on to the front of the book using double-sided tape. Cut the ribbon in half and attach a length to the inside of the front and back covers to make a tie.

Rocket Bag

This small bag uses straight stitch to bold graphic effect, with its futuristic design of space rockets, shooting stars and asteroids. It is worked in a selection of brightly coloured perlé threads on to utilitarian denim. Either side of the background fabric can be used. Each gives a different effect; the steps show the right side and the finished project shows the lighter-coloured reverse.

MATERIALS
Two 20cm (8in) squares of denim
Dressmaker's chalk or carbon
Embroidery hoop
Perlé cotton embroidery thread in a selection
  of colours
Dressmaker's pins
5 x 25cm (2 x 10in) strip of denim
Pearl button
Blue cotton sewing thread

1 Enlarge the template pattern and transfer the design on to one of the denim pieces, using dressmaker's chalk or carbon. Stretch the fabric in the embroidery hoop and fill in the main shapes of the design with satin stitch.

2 Use the outlines of the design to indicate the stitch direction. Sew parallel lines of simple running stitch to represent the trails left by the flying objects. Refer to the finished picture as a colour guide.

3 With right sides facing, pin and stitch the squares together on three sides. Press under 12mm (½in) around the open edge and hem. For the strap, fold the strip in half lengthways and stitch along the raw edge. Turn through.

4 Slip stitch the strap firmly in place on to the bag. Press the finished bag lightly. Sew the pearl button to the centre front edge of the bag. Make a buttonhole loop on the opposite side using blue cotton sewing thread.

Tea Towel

This cheerful tea towel, with its border of jaunty tea cups, may not stand up to the rigours of drying crockery. It would, however, make a lovely table cover, or would be certain to brighten a small kitchen window if used as a curtain. The cups are cut out of cotton which has been specially coloured with fabric paint and the details are added with back, cross and running stitches.

MATERIALS
Fabric paints and plain cotton fabric or
scraps of coloured fabric
Tracing paper
Dressmaker's chalk or carbon
Stranded embroidery thread in contrasting colours
Anti-fraying solution or diluted pva adhesive
Striped tea towel

1 The tea cup shapes are cut from cotton fabric. Scraps of coloured cloth would be suitable, or white fabric could be painted specially, using fabric paints. Trace the outlines from the template on to separate pieces of fabric (enlarging to fit), using dressmaker's chalk or carbon.

2 Embroider the pattern details on to the cups with three strands of embroidery thread, using straight or satin stitch. Cut out the cup shapes and tack (baste) them along the border of the tea towel in a pleasing pattern, using the main picture as a guide.

3 If the fabric has been painted, it should not unravel at the edges, but the reverse unpainted side can be coated with a specially manufactured anti-fraying solution or with diluted pva adhesive. Finally, sew the cups in place with back stitch and add extra stitched details.

House and Garden Picture

Gardeners always combined flowers and vegetables in their country plots, and this charming embroidered cottage has a flourishing garden full of both kinds of plants. Basic stitches are imaginatively used to give an added texture to the work. The feathery carrot tops and the cabbages are worked in a loose chain stitch, and the roof is stitched in irregular lines of satin stitch to suggest thatch. The house itself and the windows are outlined in back stitch and the garden is enclosed with a straight stitch picket fence.

MATERIALS
25 x 30cm (10 x 12in) piece of linen fabric
Transfer pencil or water-soluble marker pen
Tracing paper; cotton sewing thread
Stranded embroidery threads in dark and light green,
    pink, orange, red, yellow, rust and dark beige
Anti-fraying solution or diluted pva adhesive
Scraps of cotton fabric in dark and light green, pink,
    orange and red
20 x 25cm (8 x 10in) piece of cardboard
20 x 25cm (8 x 10in) picture frame

1 Transfer the house and garden outline on to the linen. This can be done by drawing freehand with a water-soluble marker pen, or by tracing the design (enlarged as required) on to tracing paper with a transfer pencil and ironing it on to the fabric. Remember to reverse the design first if using the latter method. Working with three strands of dark beige embroidery thread, back stitch over the outline of the house, garden, door and windows.

2 Using rust embroidery thread, work the roof and door in satin stitch. The door has three even rows of stitching, while the lines on the roof are less formal and more textured. Next, using dark beige embroidery thread, work a band of satin stitch across the chimney top.

3 Coat the back of the fabric scraps with a proprietary (commercial) anti-fraying solution or with diluted pva adhesive. Cut out four rough circles measuring approximately 2.5cm (1in) in diameter, from light green cotton fabric for the cabbages. Tack (baste) in place, then work the leaf markings in loose chain stitch. Stitch around the outside edge in an uneven blanket stitch.

4 Cut sixteen small carrots from orange cotton fabric. Stitch down with running stitch and sew several straight stitches across each shape. The leafy tops are worked in loose chain stitch in dark green. Work the fencing around the border to complete the garden. The flowers, stalks and leaves are cut from cotton fabric and stitched down with running stitch. Embroider a few yellow satin stitches in the centre of the petals. Lightly press the finished work from the back and stretch over the cardboard, lacing firmly at the back with cotton thread, before framing.

Folk Art Gloves

The exuberant floral motif that decorates these gloves was inspired by the patterns on an antique tablecloth from Eastern Europe. The motif has been cleverly adapted to fit on to the back of the hand and along the fingers. The two variations, working on both white and black backgrounds, show how skilful use of colour can alter the appearance of a design. The basic outline is transferred on to the glove as a guide and the embroidery is worked freehand in tapestry wool.

MATERIALS
Pair of white or black woollen gloves
Ruler; pencil; thin cardboard
Tracing paper
Dressmaker's pins
Persian tapestry wool in pink, emerald green, royal blue, dark yellow, peach, kingfisher blue, bright pink, mint green, acid green, lime green and yellow
Tapestry needle

1 To support each glove while embroidering on to it, cut narrow strips from the card to insert in the fingers and a rectangle to fit the palm. Trace the template (enlarging as necessary) and cut out around the outer edge and inner circle. Pin to the glove, matching the top of the template with the finger tips and centring the flower on the back of the hand. Mark the inner circle with a row of small pink running stitches and the dotted lines with emerald green, then remove the template by cutting away between the stitches.

2 Using pink wool, work a circle of satin stitch in the centre of the flower, using the running stitches as a guide. With peach, work a ring of stem stitch close to the inside edge of the centre circle.

3 Embroider the three leaves around the sides and base of the circle in green satin and stem stitch. Unpick the original marker stitches if they still show.

4 Using dark yellow wool, blanket stitch the outer edge of the four petals. Inside this, back stitch a line in royal blue. Fill each with a detached chain stitch, then add a ring of small satin stitches in bright pink wool.

5 Work the stamens in chain stitch, beginning each one between the markers on the centre circle and working down to 2cm (¾in) from the finger tip. Use a different shade of green wool for each one. At the top of each stamen sew a different-coloured circle by making a detached chain stitch and working over it with small satin stitches. In the centre of each circle embroider a striped bullion stitch by threading the needle with one strand each of pink and yellow yarn.

6 Finish the flower by working six bullion stitches in kingfisher blue, arranged in a star pattern to fill the centre circle. To complete, sew a two-coloured bullion stitch in the middle of these stitches.

Hairslide (Barrette)

Decorative hair accessories have always been popular. In the past women needed many pins, combs and clips to keep their elaborate hairstyles in place. These were adorned with everything from feathers, lace and flowers to beads and jewels. This oval hairslide (barrette) is covered with black satin which has been embroidered with flowing lines of silver metallic thread and a contrasting pattern of cream satin stitch. The variation is less formal in design and, with the comb, should provide inspiration for further ideas.

MATERIALS

6.5 x 10cm (2½ x 4in) oval hairslide (barrette)
Tracing paper; tissue paper
Pencil
Remnant of black satin
Embroidery hoop
Cotton sewing thread in black and white
Dressmaker's chalk or carbon; dressmaker's pins
Perlé cotton in black and cream
Silver lurex yarn
Fine silver metallic thread
Remnant of black cotton fabric
Impact adhesive
Iron-on fusible bonding

1 Copy the template, adapting it to fit the slide (barrette). Trace the grid and oval outline on to a piece of tissue paper and the oval outline and spirals on to another. Stretch the satin in the hoop and tack (baste) through the tissue with white sewing thread to mark the grid and oval, then remove the paper. Mark the outside edge with chalk 12mm (½in) from the oval outline. Embroider the diamonds alternately in black and cream satin stitch, then take out the tacking.

2 Pin the second piece of tissue paper on to the hoop, lining up the design. Use silver lurex thread for the straight stitch spiral, stitching through the paper. Tear away the tissue and use the same thread to whip over the lines to define them.

3 Use fine silver metallic thread to sew squares on to the black diamonds and black sewing cotton to embroider star stitches on to the cream. Cut out the design around the chalk line.

4 Cut a paper pattern for the backing by drawing round the slide (barrette), marking the position of the clip. Sew a gathering thread around the outside edge of the embroidered fabric and draw up slightly. Place over the slide (barrette) and adjust to fit. Pull the thread tightly, knot the ends and glue down the surplus fabric. Iron the bonding on to the black cotton fabric, then pin the pattern for the backing to this fabric and cut out the backing. Cut a slit in the backing for the clip, then stick the backing on to the slide.

Drawstring Bag

This sophisticated drawstring bag is embroidered in dark grey, cream and silver threads on two contrasting black background fabrics.

MATERIALS

30 x 90cm (12 x 36in) piece of black satin
30 x 41cm (12 x 16in) piece of black velvet
Black cotton sewing thread; contrasting sewing thread
Embroidery hoop; dressmaker's carbon or chalk
Embroidery thread in dark grey
Silver lurex thread; cream perlé embroidery thread
Fine silver metallic thread; 1.37m (1½ yd) black cord
Safety pin; dressmaker's pins

1 Enlarge the pattern. Cut one piece A from satin and one piece B from velvet for the front. Reverse the templates and repeat for the back. Cut one C from satin and one from velvet. Mark the notches. Stitch the curved edges together to form two rectangles, trim and press the seam. With contrasting thread, tack (baste) from 'a' to 'a' across the centre of each piece to mark the fold line which will eventually be the top of the bag. Work the embroidery on the lower front. Following the main picture, mark three diamonds. Outline with whipped running stitch, with six strands of grey thread.

2 Sew the two inner diamonds with silver lurex thread, using whipped running stitch. With cream crochet thread work a second diamond in straight stitch 12mm (½in) outside each silver shape and stitch a large cross in the centre of each diamond. Outline crosses with dark grey and, with the same thread, stitch a diamond around each (one long stitch per side). With metallic thread work tiny silver crosses between cream straight stitches; couch down the long stitches around crosses. Add final centre crosses with cream perlé thread. Remove from hoop and press.

3 With right sides together, stitch front and back long edges; leave four spaces between notches 'b'. Press seams and top stitch around openings. Pin, tack, then stitch velvet base C to short velvet edges of main piece; right sides together, matching notches. Stitch satin base C to short satin edges of main piece, right sides together. Leave 5cm (2in) gap in seam.

4 Turn bag right sides out through gap. Slipstitch the gap closed. Fold and press along tacked line a-a, and push satin end into velvet end to form a bag with a lining. Stitch lines at 12mm (½in) and 4cm (1½in) down from fold to make a channel for the cord, match with topstitched holes; unpick tacking. Thread cord twice through channel and stitch the two ends together.

Embroidered Hat

The embroidery on the satin brim of this elegant hat uses an interesting selection of textured threads and freestyle stitches. The spiral shapes are worked in whipped running stitch and couching, with sparkling details in metallic thread. The hat itself is made from velvet, and lined with heavy satin to match the turn-back. The coordinating scarf is made from two lengths of velvet with matching embroidery at one end.

MATERIALS

90cm (36 in) burgundy velvet
90cm (36 in) olive-green heavy satin
45cm (18 in) wide green cotton calico
Couching thread; tracing paper; pencil; tissue paper
Matching cotton sewing thread; embroidery hoop
Perlé embroidery thread in crimson and pink
Metallic thread in purple and bronze
Sewing machine; dressmaker's pins

1 Trace the pattern pieces, enlarging as necessary, then cut out in the fabrics indicated, on the bias. Cut a piece of satin 25 x 65cm (10 x 26in) for the embroidered turn-back. Trace the first part of the design on to tissue paper, including the notches in the seam allowance, and tack (baste) through on to the satin. Remove the tissue. Stretch the fabric in a hoop and, starting at the left edge, work the spirals in embroidery thread in a mixture of couched stitches and interlaced double running stitch.

2 Trace off the second part, up to the centre front. Then tack on to the satin, matching notches and marking the centre front notches. Remove the tissue. Embroider the four diamond shapes in straight and satin stitches, and the spirals in a mixture of threads.

3 Add detail to the diamonds with purple and bronze metallic thread in zigzag stitch or star shapes. Reversing the design, continue along the satin strip, moving it in the hoop, embroidering the right-hand side of the brim with the same stitches and colours as the left.

4 Press the completed embroidery. Pin calico piece C on to the back of the embroidered satin, matching notches. Cut the satin to the same shape as the calico and tack together. Join the centre back seam. Then join centre back seam of velvet piece C, pressing the seams flat. Trim the seam allowance on the velvet. Place the velvet and satin/calico with right sides together and sew along the top edge. Open out, press the seam towards the velvet, and edge-stitch through these layers, close to the seam.

5 Join the centre back seam of velvet piece B (side piece) and press open. Clip along the top edge. With right sides together, pin to velvet piece A (top of hat), matching notches. Tack, then sew together. Repeat with the two satin pieces A and B. Trim the seam allowance on the velvet and press open. Take piece C, turn the velvet over and press on the satin side. Pin together along the lower edge.

6 Pin together the lower edges of velvet pieces B and C, with pile sides together, matching the centre back seams and notches. Turn and sew together 12mm (½in) from the edge. Pin the satin lining in place with the right side facing right side of velvet (as above). Tack, then machine along 12mm (½in) seam allowance, leaving 10cm (4in) space. Pull the hat through this opening, then hand-stitch the space. Finally edge-stitch close to the seam all round to hold the satin lining in place.

Placemat

A n ordinary placemat can be changed into a conversation piece for any meal time if it is embroidered with a fanciful trompe-l'oeil place setting. The knives, forks and spoons are worked with several rows of straight stitch in gold thread. This project is a good introduction to using the sewing machine for free stitching, as the firm fabric of the mat does not need to be held within a frame and the outline is easy to follow.

MATERIALS
Ready-made woven placemat
Tissue paper; pencil; dressmaker's
  pins
Sewing machine
Machine embroidery thread in
  gold; yellow cotton sewing thread

1 Trace the cutlery designs from the template on to tissue paper, enlarging as necessary. Cut out and arrange the designs on the placemat. Pin in place.

2 Lower the feed dog on the sewing machine and change to a darning foot, using gold thread. Wind the bobbin with yellow sewing thread. Sew a line of straight stitch over the outlines.

3 Having removed the tissue paper, work four closely parallel lines of straight stitch to emphasize the outlines and decoration of the cutlery pieces. Finish off any loose ends.

Cat Picture

Machine embroidery is particularly effective when worked in solid blocks of colour. This sleeping cat is sewn in three varieties of pink, which gives the stitched surface an illusion of light and shade. The background satin stitch has been cut to give a textured tufted finish, which shows to best advantage when the picture is mounted in a deep frame.

MATERIALS
25cm (10in) square of white cotton fabric
Tracing paper; pencil
Dressmaker's chalk or carbon
Embroidery hoop
Sewing machine
Machine embroidery or sewing thread in 3 shades of the main colour and 1 background colour
Embroidery scissors
Contrasting embroidery thread

1 Trace the full-size cat outline from the template on to tracing paper. Transfer the design on to the white cotton fabric using dressmaker's chalk or carbon. Stretch the fabric in an embroidery hoop.

2 Lower the feed dog on the sewing machine and, with one shade of the main colour, fill in the outline with straight stitch. Work random lines of the other two shades of the main colour into the stitched surface, marking the paws and back leg.

3 Change the top and bottom threads on the machine to the single background colour and adjust the machine to a close zigzag. Slowly work lines of satin stitch to fill in the background, being careful not to stitch over the cat. Remove from the hoop and press lightly.

4 To obtain a textured, carpet-like background to the completed picture, use the sharp point of a pair of embroidery scissors to snip into the solid satin stitch to give a tufted surface. With three strands of contrasting embroidery thread, hand stitch the eyes, whiskers and claws.

Picture Frame

The paintings of Gustav Klimt, the Austrian symbolist artist, were the influence behind this decorative photograph frame. The jewel-like surfaces of his work are densely patterned with geometric shapes and sinuous lines, reminiscent of brocades, silks and other luxurious textiles. The embroidery is machine-worked in a free straight-stitch with a darning foot, and the fabric feed is lowered to allow a greater fluidity of movement.

MATERIALS
20 x 25cm (8 x 10in) piece of black velvet
20 x 25cm (8 x 10in) piece of metallic organza
Tissue paper; pencil; embroidery hoop
2 pieces of 15 x 20cm (6 x 8in) mounting (mat) board
Sewing machine
Machine embroidery thread in gold, cream, yellow
  and light blue
20 x 25cm (8 x 10in) piece of self-adhesive black felt
Black cotton sewing thread; pva adhesive
Short length of cord for the hanging loop

1 Trace the design from the template on to tissue paper, enlarging as required. Layer the tissue, organza and velvet and tack together across the centre and then around the edges. Stretch the fabric in a hoop.

2 Thread the machine with gold thread and use a darning foot. Lower the feed dog and set to straight stitch, then sew along the wavy lines and around the triangles, moving the frame as necessary.

3 Tear off the tissue paper and fill in the triangles with rows of straight stitch, using the various coloured threads. Thread all the loose ends of cotton to the back of the work.

4 Cut a rectangle from the centre of one of the pieces of mounting (mat) cardboard, to leave a 3.5cm (1½in) wide frame. Place on the reverse of the embroidery and cut out the middle section, leaving a 12mm (½in) seam allowance.

5 Mitre the corners of the frame, then fold the edges to the back and pull together with large stitches, making sure that the corners are tidy Take the second piece of board and cover with self-adhesive felt.

6 Glue the board to the frame along the two sides and bottom edge, so that the picture can be inserted from the top. Attach a short length of cord to the back of the frame to make a hanging loop, or make a simple stand from a triangle of cardboard which has been covered with black felt.

Fish Mobile

Shimmering gauzes and translucent organzas (organdy) give a wonderfully watery feel to this mobile, which would look equally at home in the bathroom or the nursery. The seahorses, fish and seaweed are worked in metallic machine embroidery threads on to water-soluble fabric. This special technique means that fine, net-like fabrics can be created, which are ideally suited to the seaside theme.

MATERIALS

Water-soluble fabric; indelible felt-tip pen; tracing paper; pen; embroidery hoop; sewing machine
Assortment of crystalline and metallic organzas (organdies), tinsel and other shiny fabrics; dressmaker's pins
Matching metallic machine embroidery threads
60cm (24in) length of 12mm (1/2in) dowelling
Blue and green diluted craft paints
Nylon fishing line; clear glass beads

1 Copy the templates for the fish, seaweed and seahorse, enlarging as necessary. Trace a fish and a frond of seaweed on to water-soluble fabric and put into the hoop. Cut two scraps of organza and sandwich small fragments of metallic fabrics between them for the body. Pin to the underside of hoop. Thread machine with metallic thread, lower feed dog and set to straight stitch. Sew around the main body and head.

2 Work the seaweed in the same way as step 1, using matching green thread and green organza. Extra freedom in stitching can be achieved by removing the presser foot on the sewing machine, but this way of working demands special care in handling the hoop, and is not absolutely necessary.

3 Turn the embroidery hoop over and trim back the excess fabric, then, to complete the fish, work the main fins and tail by outlining them with a zigzag stitch, filling in the space with interlacing lines of straight stitch. Work the two separate fins in the same way, then work a frilly zigzag stitch around the seaweed.

4 Dip the completed pieces of the mobile into water and allow the water-soluble backing fabric to dissolve. Rinse the pieces carefully to remove any traces of the backing fabric, then dry each on a towel, away from direct heat.

5 Following the same method, make eight extra lengths of seaweed, two seahorses and four more fish. Alter the shape and colour schemes so that the fish are all different. Attach each fish to a piece of fishing line, varying the lengths. Twist seaweed around the line and sew in place.

6 Cut the dowel into one 25cm (10in) and two 18cm (7in) lengths and stain with the craft paint. Stitch the seaweed to the dowel as shown. Hang the mobile and adjust so that it is evenly balanced. Sew glass beads to the fish and seaweed, to add both extra weight and decoration.

Table Cloth

Water-soluble fabric can be adapted to a variety of uses when embroidering with the sewing machine. It is usually used as a foundation for making net-like fabrics, but it also serves as an effective support when two materials of very different weights are being used. For this project, delicate openwork motifs in pearly white organza (organdy) are set into a heavy linen table cloth to make an attractive centrepiece.

MATERIALS
Dressmaker's chalk or carbon
Linen table cloth
Tissue paper
30 x 60cm (12 x 24in) piece of white organza (organdy)
30 x 60cm (12 x 24in) piece of water-soluble fabric
Dressmaker's pins
White cotton sewing thread; sewing machine
Embroidery hoop; sharp embroidery scissors

1 With dressmaker's chalk or carbon draw out a 20cm (8in) square centrally on the reverse side of the table cloth. Trace the cut-out design on to tissue paper and use the main picture as a guide to setting out the motifs. Cut a piece of organza (organdy) and water-soluble fabric to size and line up along one side of the square. Pin the tissue paper on top.

2 Thread the machine with white thread, lower the feed dog and put on a darning foot. Place the fabric in an embroidery hoop. Following the marked line, straight stitch around the motif, then remove the tissue paper.

3 Turn the cloth over and, with sharp scissors, cut away the linen from inside the shape, taking care not to snip through either the outline stitches or the organza.

4 Set the machine to a wide close satin stitch and sew over the straight stitch line enclosing the raw edges. Work the other four sides of the square in the same way, then wash away the water-soluble fabric in cold water. Allow to dry, then press.

Needlepoint

Needlepoint involves working stitches on to a canvas to create geometric or illustrative designs. Its simplicity means that it is growing in popularity, and only a needle, some yarn and a piece of canvas are required to get started. Many ready-to-work kits are available, but, with some knowledge, it is easy to create individual pieces, from simple tent stitch pictures to elaborate textured cushions (pillows).

Needlepoint

The popular craft of needlepoint is also known as tapestry, canvas work and canvas embroidery. The formal stitches are worked on to a geometric canvas grid, using various scales; stranded embroidery silks on fine canvas give a lustrous, detailed result, while several strands of woollen yarn can be worked together on a thick rug canvas.

The first large pieces of needlepoint were made in imitation of the expensive and sought-after tapestries that were hand-woven in specialist workshops in Britain and Europe. They were worked in a single stitch on fine canvas to give the appearance of the densely woven texture of true tapestry, and some of the stitch names, such as "Gobelin filling", after the French tapestry studio, reflect this. The most popular stitch was tent stitch, and this is still most commonly used for pictorial work, particularly ready-to-work kits. It produces a durable surface, which can last for many years.

Needlepoint has always been the most practical form of embroidery and the most hard-wearing, which means that much of it has survived the centuries. The ornamental court dress and other embroidered clothing of the

Elizabethan era was recycled when it became unfashionable. Pearls, beads and jewels were reused, gold thread was taken out and tassels unravelled. Many needlepoint items from that time, however, were preserved, including panels believed to have been worked by the Queen herself. Bible covers, often featuring scenes from the Old and New Testaments, were made to protect precious printed books from wear, and purses or bags were made as gifts. These often featured mottoes, along with the emblematic and symbolic devices that fascinated the Elizabethans.

Illustrated pattern books first appeared on the market in sixteenth century Europe, and these provided a vast resource for professional and amateur designers. One of the earliest has the engaging title: *A Book of Beasts, Birds, Flowers, Fruits, Flies and Wormes, exactly drawne with their Lively Colours truly Described,* which gives a graphic impression of the outline designs contained in it. Samplers were often made to try out some of these patterns, but the early versions were purely practice pieces worked on long strips of fabric, not framed for display, like later work.

In addition to small items,

A carefully thought-out selection of needlepoint stitches has been used to embroider this classically proportioned house, its garden and its background.

This modern reworking of an antique charted pattern gives some impression of just how bright Victorian needlework was originally meant to be.

Ready-made kits, such as this duck cushion (pillow), are screen printed on to canvas. A separate screen is made for each of the colours in the design and the inks carefully matched to the yarns.

needlepoint was widely used for furnishings, from wall hangings and bed draperies to cushion (pillow) covers and footstools. In the days before padded upholstery, when all furniture was made from wood, soft cushions (pillows) were a necessary comfort. Floor coverings and rugs were also made, although these were not intended for everyday use, and special table carpets were made to drape over dining tables when not in use. These furnishings, usually worked in tent stitch, were decorated with biblical or mythical scenes and drew heavily on heraldic imagery. Trade links between the East and Europe were growing throughout the seventeenth century and as new and exotic textiles were imported, their designs were adapted for needlepoint.

For many years, needlepoint was used simply to copy paintings and engravings. It was not until the nineteenth century that it came into its own with the spread of Berlin woolwork. This was worked in cross or tent stitch from printed charts, which first appeared in Germany in 1805. Black and white engravings, which used tiny symbols to represent different yarns, were hand-painted to give a full range of colour. Small numbers of designs were imported during the early years of the nineteenth century but it was with the invention of the first chemical or aniline dyes in the mid-nineteenth century that Berlin woolwork became widely popular. New textile technology meant that, for the first time, yarns could be manufactured in vivid hues – purple, emerald, crimson, lime greens and acid yellows – that could not have been achieved with natural dyes. Many of the old charts have survived and give some idea of just how bright Victorian needlework really was. The colours have faded over the years, and many antique pieces have a worn and nostalgic look that belies their original appearance.

Ladies of leisure set about adorning their homes with bell-pulls, footstools, firescreens and pictures and making smoking caps, braces (suspenders) and slippers for their menfolk. Patterns ranged from representational romantic landscapes, through realistic bowls of flowers to outrightly sentimental portraits of the royal princes and princesses and even the Queen's pets. Some of the designs were very complicated and intricate and the Countess of Wilton, writing in 1840, bemoaned the fact that many women optimistically bought charts and yarns, then found that they could not easily work them – a not uncommon complaint today.

Tent stitch pictures will always be popular, but needlepoint has now evolved into an independent branch of embroidery, with many stitches – both traditional and modern variations – which can be combined to give an enormous range of effects, patterns, styles and textures.

Fruit, acorn, butterfly and flower motifs from an Elizabethan pattern book were the inspiration for this enchanting tent stitch design.

Needlepoint
Tools and Materials

Needlepoint, or canvas work, is the craft of stitching on to a firm open-weave square mesh or canvas, as opposed to the softer background fabrics used for embroidery. It is traditionally worked with wool, although many different yarns can be used to produce interesting effects.

THREADS
4-ply tapestry and 2-ply crewel yarns are both available in skeins or hanks, in a full range of colours. Vivid Persian yarn comes in three separate strands which can be divided.

Persian yarns.

CANVAS
Like embroidery linen, canvas is gauged by the number of threads that make up 2.5cm (1in): 10-count canvas is used for most tent stitch, rug canvas has just three squares to 2.5cm (1in) and fine 22-count fabric is used with single crewel yarns. Light-coloured canvas is suitable for working with pale colours, but antique or undyed canvas should be chosen for darker yarns so that it does not show through.

Mono, or single-thread canvas is available in a wide range of gauges for traditional needlepoint: for best results use interlock canvas which has a twisted warp and therefore does not pull out of shape easily. Double, or Penelope canvas is woven with pairs of thread, for tramming, which can also be sub-divided for areas of smaller stitching. Plastic canvas is sold by the sheet and can be cut to shape with scissors. It does not distort and is ideal for making three-dimensional shapes.

TOOLS AND ACCESSORIES
To avoid large pieces of work becoming distorted, a rectangular stretcher frame or an adjustable scroll frame must be used to mount the canvas. For smaller projects, the canvas can be simply bound with masking tape to prevent it unravelling and, if necessary, blocked into shape when complete.

A tapestry needle has a large eye for easy threading and a blunt point to pass between the canvas threads. Tapestry needles come in different sizes ranging from number 13 for coarse work, to the most common, number 20, down to the finest, number 25.

Both large and small scissors will be needed to cut canvas and yarns and a marker pen or acrylic paints are used to transfer designs directly on to the working canvas.

Crewel and tapestry yarns.

Embroidery scissors.

Acrylic paints with paint mixe

Plastic canvas.

Double or Penelope canvas of different gauges.

Interlock canvas of different gauges.

Single or mono canvas.

Dressmaker's shears.

Tapestry needles.

Permanent marker pen.

Masking tape.

Tapestry or scroll frame.

Creating the Design

T he scope for creating new designs is unlimited. Visual inspiration is all around: a single motif from a furnishing fabric can be adapted to make a co-ordinating cushion (pillow), or used on a smaller scale as an all-over repeat; a photograph of an exotic flower may suggest a representational tent stitch picture or a more abstract colour pattern, worked in textured stitches. It is important to bear in mind the scale of the finished piece – for a fast result, bold shapes can be worked on 7-count canvas with three strands of Persian yarn, but for fine detail 12- or 14-count canvas should be used with crewel or tapestry wool. Try combining stitches: tent stitch is good for details and fine lines, while decorative stitches will cover background areas more quickly.

DRAWING ON TO CANVAS

This Gothic Revival pattern has been traced directly on to the canvas, using a waterproof felt-tip pen. The canvas should be placed directly over the drawing. Be sure that the design is squared up correctly. This can be done by ruling horizontal and vertical guides to indicate the centre of the canvas and matching them with similar lines marked on the design. Tape the canvas in place before starting to draw.

1 MAKING CHARTS
The regular grid of graph paper resembles the mesh of woven canvas, which makes charting an ideal way to produce accurate needlepoint designs. It is particularly good for tent stitch patterns, where one coloured square represents one stitch. Match the scale of the paper to the canvas for easier working, e.g., 12-count paper to 12-count canvas.

PAINTING ON TO CANVAS
Highly detailed designs can be painted directly on to canvas using textile paints, which are then ironed to fix the colour. This technique works best on "antique" canvas which is made of unbleached fibres.

2 Choose a design that has a strong shape and solid blocks of colour. Trace the outline with a soft pencil and transfer on to graph paper.

3 Using the original picture as a guide, colour in the squares, simplifying the most complicated shapes.

Working with Colour

Almost any type of thread can be used for needlepoint. Metallic yarns and silk floss provide highlights within a design; heavy-duty rug yarn is suitable for large-scale canvases, and perlé or stranded embroidery threads give a smooth lustrous texture. Woollen yarns are, however, the most popular choice, especially for items that will receive a lot of wear. A wide range of colours is available, from several specialist manufacturers. The yarn is spun from specially selected fibres, which make it more durable than knitting wool. Needlepoint wools come in three main types: tapestry yarn, crewel wool and Persian yarn. The first is a 4-ply single-strand yarn, supplied in skeins or larger hanks, which is used on medium canvases. Crewel wool is a 2-ply single strand yarn and can be worked singly on fine-mesh canvas for the most detailed work, or with several strands combined. Four strands are the equivalent of tapestry yarn. Persian yarn is also 2-ply and consists of three fine strands, which can easily be separated. The thread chosen for any work must cover the canvas threads completely without being so thick that it cannot be pulled through easily. Sew with a length of about 45cm (18in) to prevent the yarn becoming frayed or knotted.

1 By combining several separate strands of either crewel or Persian yarn, an infinite number of hues can be created. This can give depth to a representational image or, as here, be an excuse to work in bands of pure colour. The selection of yarns is based on the richly shaded landscape of the Channel Islands.

2 To blend the colours, cut equal lengths from the skeins and separate the strands.

3 Thread the needle with two contrasting or closely shaded yarns and work as usual. Up to four strands can be used on wider-mesh canvases; if all of these are different, some stunning results can be produced.

Left: The patterns on well-worn cotton print fabrics are the inspiration for this patchwork hand and heart. The subtle faded colours are reproduced by working with closely matched shades of Persian tapestry yarns.

This simple geometric design is based on the Saw-tooth Star quilt motif and worked in two strands of crewel yarn on a fine canvas. The changes in colour give a lively appearance to the pattern surface.

Starting and Finishing

Needlepoint's popularity comes from the fact that only the most basic equipment is needed, there are no special techniques to be learned and it is quick to work. The yarn must be started and ended correctly, and an even tension maintained. This will come with experience, so it is worth practising a few stitches on spare canvas.

1 PREPARING THE CANVAS The canvas should be bound with masking tape to prevent the edges unravelling and to stop the yarn from catching. If a frame is not being used, the sides of a large piece of work can be rolled up, so that only the area being stitched shows.

2 GETTING STARTED The end of the wool should not simply be knotted and pulled to the right side, as in embroidery, because it can easily become untied or work through the canvas. Instead the needle is passed through from the front, a short distance from the starting point, then brought up from the back. When the surplus yarn has been stitched over, the knot can be snipped off.

3 FINISHING OFF The yarn is finished on the wrong side. Bring the needle through and weave it under the back of the finished stitches for about 2.5cm (1in). Trim the end. Try not to start and end the threads in the same place: this can make the work uneven.

BLOCKING

Most needlepoint stitches are diagonal, so the square weave of the canvas is bound to get pulled out of line during sewing. This is less likely to happen if the work has been supported on a frame, but some distortion is inevitable. The finished piece should be very lightly pressed from the wrong side with a steam iron, but may need to be "blocked" to restore its intended shape.

1 Dampen the work thoroughly on both sides, using a water spray.

2 Place a protective piece of plastic under the canvas, then pin down the first corner. Stretch the canvas and secure the opposite corner. Pull the work into shape and pin down the other two corners.

3 Push more drawing pins (thumb tacks) into the unstitched canvas, and use a ruler or set square to check the right angles at each corner. Leave to dry away from any direct source of heat.

Tent Stitch

Tent stitch, sometimes known as petit point, is the most flexible of all needlepoint stitches. It produces an even texture, and can be worked in large blocks of solid colour or used for shading effects and fine detail. It is worked diagonally, with all the stitches lying in the same direction. There are three different ways of forming the stitch: half cross stitch, continental stitch and basketweave stitch.

The reverse of these canvases shows the differences between the three methods of working tent stitch. Left to right: half cross stitch, continental stitch, basketweave stitch.

HALF CROSS STITCH

This must be worked on double or interlocked canvas to prevent the stitches slipping. Although it resembles continental stitch from the front, half cross stitch is worked quite differently, and using both stitches in one piece gives an irregular surface.

1 Start at the top left and work each row from left to right. Bring the needle through and take it up to the right over one intersection, then back down under one horizontal thread and out to start the next stitch.

2 Turn the canvas upside down, and work the next row in the same way.

TRAMMED TENT STITCH
Worked on double thread canvas, over a long foundation stitch, this method gives a slightly ridged and very resilient surface, which is traditionally used for stools or chair seats.

Left: Cushion (pillow) covers, which need to be hard-wearing, are usually worked in tent stitch.

CONTINENTAL STITCH

This second horizontal method can be used on single canvas, but uses slightly more thread than half cross stitch.

1 Starting at top right of the canvas, bring the needle out and up to the right, over one intersection. Insert it through the canvas, down under two horizontal threads and out to the front, and repeat to the end of the row.

2 Next, turn the work upside down and work all subsequent rows in the same way.

BASKETWEAVE STITCH

This diagonal way of working produces a stronger stitch which does not distort the canvas as much as the horizontal methods, but does tend to use more wool.

1 Work the first row from left to right. Pull the needle through and take it up to the right, over one intersection, then bring it back to the front, from under two horizontal threads.

2 Work the return row upwards from right to left, inserting the stitches in the spaces left from the first row.

Diagonal Stitches

O ver the years many different needlepoint stitches have evolved and entire stitch dictionaries have been devoted to explaining them. They can be broken down, however, into just a few basic groups: diagonal stitches, straight stitches, square stitches, and variations on cross and star stitches. The diagonal stitches are useful background or filling stitches, ideal for covering large areas. They can be sewn in a single colour to give a smooth brocade-like surface, or in stripes for a more dramatic effect. The method of working means that there is a diagonal pull on the canvas, so the finished piece tends to become distorted.

From top to bottom: Moorish, Jacquard and Byzantine stitch.

BYZANTINE STITCH

This consists of diagonal zigzag rows, which can be worked over two, three or four intersections of the canvas. The size of each "step" can be varied, but should remain constant within the piece.

Work four diagonal stitches over two intersections, from left to right, then four stitches downwards. Repeat to form the zigzag, then work the subsequent rows in parallel. Fill in any space with graduated diagonal stitches.

JACQUARD STITCH

This is made up of two repeated zigzags. The basic stepped row of Byzantine stitch is worked over two intersections and followed by a row of tent stitch.

Stitch the first stepped row as before, then work the second line in diagonal stitches over one intersection, across, and then down the canvas.

MOORISH STITCH

Here the square elements of cushion (pillow) stitch are combined with zigzag lines. If Moorish stitch is worked in two colours, it produces a geometric checked pattern.

1 The first row consists of diagonal stitches worked over one, two, three, four, then three, two and one intersections.

2 Work a line of stepped stitches over two intersections to fit alongside the first row and repeat these two rows.

From left to right: small diagonal mosaic stitch, condensed Scottish stitch and Milanese stitch.

SMALL DIAGONAL MOSAIC STITCH

Also known as Parisian stitch, this is made by following a tent stitch over one intersection with a longer stitch over two intersections. Work the sequence along a diagonal of the canvas, and work the next row so that it fits beside the first. It can be worked from right to left or left to right.

MILANESE STITCH

Diagonal rows of triangles facing in opposite directions make up this stitch, and it is particularly effective when worked in two colours.

1 Work diagonal stitches over one, two, three and four intersections to form a triangle, then repeat the unit.

2 The second row is reversed, so that the shortest stitch fits next to the longest stitch of the first row.

CONDENSED SCOTTISH STITCH

This resembles parallel lines of interlocked diamond shapes and gives a strong diagonal appearance.

1 Work a unit of graduated stitches over two, three, four, and then three intersections. Repeat this along the diagonal.

2 Work the same sequence for the next row, interlocking the two lines so that the shortest stitch of one row fits against the longest. stitch of the adjacent row.

Square Stitches

This category includes diagonal, upright and horizontal elements, creating repeated square units, a chequerboard effect, and interesting variations when using more than one colour.

SMALL CUSHION (PILLOW) STITCH

Also known as mosaic stitch. When worked in a single colour, as in the finished sample, it gives an overall texture. Several colours produce a quite different effect.

1 Start at the upper left and work diagonally downwards over first one, then two, intersections.

2 The following rows are worked up, then back down, so that each line fits into the previous stitches.

SCOTTISH STITCH

This gives a plaid effect, reminiscent of simple tartan patterns, which looks very effective when worked in contrasting yarns.

1 Work the grid first, using horizontal and vertical rows of tent stitch with a three- or four-thread space left between them.

2 Fill in the spaces with individual cushion (pillow) stitches.

From left to right: cushion (pillow) stitch, small cushion (pillow) stitch and Scottish stitch.

CUSHION (PILLOW) STITCH

This can be worked so that all the squares lie in the same direction, or at an angle to each other, which reduces the tension on the canvas.

1 This basic square is made up from seven stitches over one, two, three, four, three, two, then one intersections, worked in diagonal rows. For two-colour work, leave four thread spaces between rows.

2 Diagonal rows of the second colour are used to fill in the spaces.

CHEQUER (CHECKER) STITCH

This alternates small squares of tent stitch with lines of graduated diagonal stitch to produce an interesting texture, particularly when two colours are used.

1 Work diagonal lines of cushion (pillow) stitch squares over four threads.

2 With the second colour, work four rows of four tent stitches to fill in the spaces.

WOVEN STITCH

This stitch produces an intriguing basketweave effect, which appears to have been interwoven. It can also be worked in just one colour.

1 Working from right to left, make blocks of three parallel straight stitches over four threads, leaving a three- or four-thread space between. Work the next row so that the blocks lie immediately below the spaces above.

2 The second colour is used to fill in the spaces. Starting from the top right, work blocks of upright straight stitches over four threads, so that the first and last stitches of each block overlap the horizontal stitches from the first row.

BRIGHTON STITCH

This is worked in alternate rows of diagonal stitches which form a diamond pattern. The small spaces are filled in with upright cross stitch.

1 Start with a block of five diagonal stitches worked from left to right, then a second block slanting the other way. Work the next row so that it is a mirror image of the first.

2 Work an upright cross stitch, in the same or in a contrasting colour, over the two threads which have been left unworked between the stitches.

From left to right: woven stitch, Brighton stitch and chequer (checker) stitch.

Crossed Stitches

T he foundation of this group is the simple
cross stitch, which is made from two
diagonal stitches crossing in the centre. Other
variations may combine upright and horizontal
stitches, and consist of repeated units of two or
four stitches. Crossed stitches should always be
sewn in the same order, so that the upper
stitches lie in the same direction.

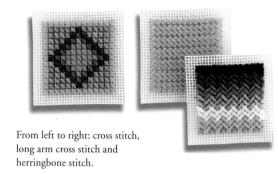

From left to right: cross stitch,
long arm cross stitch and
herringbone stitch.

CROSS STITCH

This can be worked singly, or in rows when larger areas need
to be covered. When small stitches, covering a single
intersection, are required, they should be worked on a
double or interlock canvas.

1 Individual cross stitches are
worked from right to left, then
from left to right. Bring out the
needle and take it up to the left over
two intersections. Push through the
canvas, pass down behind two
threads and bring it up. Work the
second stitch over the first and bring
the needle back to the starting point
of the second stitch.

2 When working in rows, make
the crosses in two passes. Form
the lower stitches by sewing from
right to left. Bring the needle out and
up to the left over two intersections,
and under two horizontal threads.
Repeat to the end.

3 For the upper stitches, work a
line of separate diagonal
stitches in the same way, reversing
the direction so that they cover the
first line.

LONG ARM CROSS STITCH

Also known as Greek stitch, the long arm cross stitch forms a
braid-like line, made by the stitches crossing off centre. It
can be used singly as a border or in rows for a solid texture.

Work from left to right. Bring the
needle up over two threads and four
threads to the right to make a long
diagonal stitch. Insert under two
horizontal threads and bring up. Take
up to the left, over two intersections,
then insert under two horizontal
threads and bring up. Repeat both
stitches to the end of the row.

HERRINGBONE STITCH

This produces a dense woven look, particularly effective
when worked in stripes of tonal colours.

1 Starting at the upper left and
working from left to right, bring
the needle out and down diagonally
to the right over four intersections.
Pass left under two threads, then up
diagonally right over four
intersections. Pass the needle left
under two vertical threads and bring
out. Repeat to the end.

2 Start the next row and
subsequent rows two thread
spaces below the first stitch. Work
the stitch as before, so that the rows
interlock.

OBLONG STITCH VARIATION

This is made up of rows of longer stitches, which are held in place with small back stitches.

1 The base row is worked as for normal cross stitch, but the stitches are formed over four horizontal and two vertical threads.

2 Using a matching or contrasting thread, make a row of back stitches over the two vertical threads in the centre of each stitch.

RICE STITCH

This very attractive stitch covers the canvas completely. Each stitch unit consists of a cross stitch which is held down at each corner with a grain-like back stitch.

1 Work rows of large cross stitches over four intersections.

2 Using a contrasting colour, make four back stitches in a diamond shape over each cross.

DOUBLE STRAIGHT CROSS STITCH

This forms a raised diamond consisting of four separate stitches (two crosses). Each unit is worked separately and the same order of construction must always be followed to give a regular appearance.

1 Bring the needle up and over four horizontal threads. Pass behind under two intersections, out and over four vertical threads to form a large cross. Bring up at the left, through the space that lies between the two arms.

2 Form a second cross by taking the needle down over two intersections, behind and to the left under two vertical threads, then up to the right over two intersections.

From top to bottom: oblong stitch variation, double straight cross stitch, and rice stitch.

Star Stitches

S tars combine diagonal and straight lines to produce bold dramatic shapes which look particularly effective when worked in rows of complementary colours. They are used to create definite shapes and patterns, rather than to fill in backgrounds or large areas.

ALGERIAN EYE STITCH
Made up of 16 stitches radiating from a centre point, this should be worked in a thickish thread with a fairly loose tension, so that the canvas is covered.

1 Each stitch is worked over four threads. Bring the needle up at the centre, then insert it to the left over four threads, and pull back up through the original space. Count two threads down and four across for the second stitch. Make the third stitch over four intersections down to the left, the fourth over four horizontal threads and two vertical ones. Continue, working counter-clockwise, until the whole square has been covered.

2 Further stitches can be worked in horizontal or vertical rows. Lines of back stitch, over two threads, surround the finished stitches.

RAY STITCH
Also known as fan stitch, this consists of five stitches and resembles one corner of Algerian eye stitch. Its lively appearance comes from working each row in opposite directions.

Bring the needle through and take it down over four threads, then back to the starting point. Count down four threads and two threads to the left for the second stitch, then work the third stitch over four intersections to the left. Count up two for the fourth stitch, and work back over four threads, then work the final stitch at right angles to the first.

From top to bottom: ray stitch, Algerian eye stitch and Rhodes stitch.

RHODES STITCH
This is usually worked on a single canvas to produce a raised, highly textured surface. All the stitches are worked in the same direction so that they match.

1 Bring the thread through, then count six threads to the right and four down. Insert the needle and bring back up one hole below the starting point and insert again, one hole above the end of the first stitch.

2 Continue working counter-clockwise in this way, until the whole six-thread square has been covered.

Straight Stitches

Straight stitches lie parallel with the weave and are usually worked on a single canvas so that the threads are covered completely. The most interesting variation is Florentine or flame stitch, used for Bargello work. This historic technique has long been popular, particularly in Italy. It is worked in repeated rows of an elaborate zigzag, and there are many variations on the basic pattern.

CHEVRON STITCH
This gives a strong horizontal zigzag pattern. Work over three to five threads to give wider or narrower bands.

1 Over four threads, work four straight lines, starting each stitch one hole up to the right, then work three stitches sloping downwards. Continue to the end of the row.

2 Work the second row in the same way, so that the chevrons fit neatly together.

HUNGARIAN DIAMOND STITCH
A good filling stitch that can be worked in a single colour. The height of the stitches may be varied. Work a diamond shape of vertical stitches over two, four, six and four horizontal threads. Repeat to the end of the row. Work the next rows in the same way, with the longest stitch below the shortest stitch of the previous row.

FLORENTINE STITCH
This is quick to work: once the first line has been stitched, the subsequent rows repeat the same series of peaks and valleys. Shades of the same colour can be used to give an antique feel to the work.

UPRIGHT GOBELIN STITCH
This resembles the ridged surface of hand-woven tapestries and is named after the work produced by the Gobelin family's factory in Paris.

Work from right to left, then from left to right. Bring the needle through, pass it down over two, three or four horizontal threads, then back up to form the next stitch.

GOBELIN FILLING STITCH
This can be used to produce subtle shaded effects, and can be worked in different lengths. The overlapping rows give a smooth surface.

Work a row of vertical stitches over six horizontal threads, leaving one row of holes between them. Work the next row between these stitches, starting three threads down from the top of the preceding row.

Clockwise from top: chevron stitch, Hungarian diamond stitch, Gobelin filling stitch and upright Gobelin stitch.

Jewellery Box

The soft, natural earth colours of this jewellery box echo the subtle, faded shades which are typical of old textiles. A simple outline for the pattern itself is given here, however, the actual yarns used can be chosen almost at random, and then blended together for an informal effect. The plastic canvas used for the lid is ideal for constructing three-dimensional objects; it is simple to cut to any size and strong enough to hold its shape.

MATERIALS

12.5 x 20cm (5 x 8in) piece of plastic canvas
Waterproof felt-tip pen
Tapestry yarn in a selection of toning colours
Tapestry needle
36 x 90cm (14 x 36in) piece of self-adhesive black felt
30cm (12in) square of sturdy cardboard
Metal ruler
Cutting board
Craft knife

1 Cut the box lid sections from the plastic canvas: one 12.5cm (5in) square, and four 2 x 12.5cm (¾ x 5in) rectangles to form the sides. Enlarge then trace the template on to the canvas with a waterproof pen. Work the design in tent stitch, blending the colours using two toning strands.

2 Sew the four side pieces of the fold in the same way as step 1, then overstitch the long edges to the square using two different colours of yarn in the needle. Join the short edges to complete the lid.

3 Overstitch the raw edges of the canvas to make a neat border. Cut an 18cm (7in) square of self-adhesive black felt to line the box lid. Clipping the corners to fit, peel off the backing paper and stick in place, trimming the lower edge as necessary.

4 To make the main box, mark a 11.5cm (4½in) square in the centre of the cardboard. Then on each side rule a 9 x 11.5cm (3½ x 4½in) rectangle. Cut out the cross shape and score along the folds.

5 Using this shape as a guide, cut out two pieces of black felt for the inside and outside of the box, each with tabs on the four sides and 12mm(½in) turn-over around the top edge on one piece.

6 Fold the cardboard along the scored lines and cover the outside with the felt, using the tabs to secure the corners and folding over at the top. Use the second piece of felt to line the inside of the box.

Lone-Star Cushion (Pillow)

This needlepoint cushion (pillow) is an adaptation of an Amish patchwork bedcover design from the 1930s and reflects their mastery of colour. Its strong graphic impact relies upon the interaction of light and dark shades in muted tones, which radiate from the centre in concentric rings. The design is worked in a diagonal stitch, which gives it an almost padded effect, suggesting the quilted patterns of the original cover.

MATERIALS
41cm (16in) square of 12-count single-thread canvas
Masking tape; tapestry needle; cotton sewing thread
Tapestry frame (optional)
Tapestry yarn:
  1 skein each in pale lilac, dark peach, indigo, orange,
    crimson and dark gold
  2 skeins in light turquoise
  6 skeins in dark turquoise
  6 skeins in dark purple
Matching velvet or needlecord fabric for the backing
30cm (12in) cushion (pillow) pad

1 Bind the edges of the canvas with masking tape to prevent them unravelling. Find the middle of the canvas by folding it in half each way and sew two rows of tacking stitch in contrasting thread to divide it into quarters. Mount the canvas on a frame if desired. Using the tacking lines as a guide, stitch the centre star in pale lilac yarn, working diagonally over four threads of canvas, Following the chart, sew the next round in dark purple.

2 Work the next four rounds in dark peach, indigo, dark turquoise, then light turquoise, and then continue with the dark purple round that starts to divide the points of the star, carrying the thread behind the work.

3 Using the picture as a guide, work the points, starting and finishing each colour separately. Fill the dark turquoise background in diagonal stitch.

4 Work a border of three lines of dark purple diagonal stitch, in the direction of the previous stitches. Stretch and block the work into shape, then cut a 33cm (13in) square of backing fabric. With right sides together, join to the canvas on three sides, turn right way out, insert the cushion (pillow) pad and slip stitch the final side closed.

Nine-Star Cushion (Pillow)

The nine-star is a variation of the distinctive lone-star quilt design. The basic unit is an eight-pointed star, which is repeated in three rows of three, to produce an interesting secondary pattern of squares and diamonds. The stars are worked in complementary faded tones of burgundy, rust and pinks, in diagonal stitch, and the cream background in textured cushion (pillow) stitch.

MATERIALS

41cm (16in) square of 12-count single-thread canvas
Masking tape; cotton sewing thread; tapestry needle
Tapestry frame (optional)
Tapestry yarn:
* 8 skeins in cream*
* 1 skein each in pale lemon and light gold*
* 2 skeins each in pale pink, rust and burgundy*
* 3 skeins each in dark pink and dark gold*
Toning fabric for the backing
30cm (12in) cushion (pillow) pad

1 Bind the outside edge of the canvas with masking tape to prevent it fraying. Mark the middle of the canvas with two lines of running stitch in contrasting thread, then mount on a frame if desired. Use the guides to position the centre star. Following the chart, work the first round with pale lemon yarn, using a diagonal stitch over three threads of canvas. Work the next two rounds in light gold and pale pink.

2 Stitch the next round in dark pink, then work the tapering diamond points following the main photograph. Find the position of the four stars around the centre star by stitching the diamonds at their tips, where they touch the outer points of the first star.

3 Work the four corner stars in the same way. Fill in the background with cushion (pillow) stitch squares using cream yarn. Work the other eight diamonds, then stitch a final row of cushion (pillow) stitch around the edge. Stretch and block the finished piece. Cut the backing fabric to the same size and sew together round three edges, with right sides facing. Turn the right way out, insert the cushion (pillow) pad and slip stitch the fourth side closed.

Heart Picture

The heart is the ultimate symbol of love and affection, and as such recurs throughout the applied arts of many cultures. For this dramatic tent stitch panel, one basic motif is repeated six times, in a format influenced by the Pop Art screen prints of Andy Warhol. The vibrant colour comes from blending individual strands of Persian yarn, which is dyed in particularly intense hues.

1 Plan the colour combinations before starting to sew. Choose complementary shades for subtle backgrounds, such as the pale blue and lilac square, and contrasting tones – lime and emerald green – for more impact.

2 Separate the yarn into strands and, working with two strands at a time, work the heart motifs in tent stitch. Follow the chart, on which one square represents one stitch.

3 Vary the colour within some individual shapes; two different pinks are used for the final heart. Plastic canvas has the great advantage that it does not need to be blocked into shape, so it is suited to work that will be framed. Trim the finished piece to fit the frame using sharp scissors.

MATERIALS
Persian yarn in a selection of pinks, reds, blues and greens
Tapestry needle
11.5 x 15cm (4½ x 6in) piece of 10-count plastic canvas
7.5 x 11.5cm (3 x 4½in) picture frame
Embroidery scissors

Circular Star

Plastic canvas is available in round shapes of various sizes, as well as in the more usual square grid pattern. This gives great scope for experimentation with designs based on the geometric division of a circle. Stars and snowflake motifs naturally lend themselves to this, and make unusual Christmas decorations. The scale of this project makes it a good way to use up small amounts of yarn. Use the photograph as a stitching guide.

MATERIALS
7.5cm (3in) diameter plastic canvas disc
Waterproof felt-tip pen (optional)
Tapestry needle
Tapestry wool yarn in a selection of toning colours
Small piece of self-adhesive felt
30cm (12in) length of satin ribbon

1 Copy the star design from the template. (The pattern could be traced directly on to the canvas with a waterproof felt-tip pen.) Thread the needle with two different coloured yarns to create a mottled effect. Stitch one-quarter of the design at a time, working from the centre outwards. To secure the ends of the yarn do not knot them, but leave a length and catch under the back when stitching.

2 Using the main picture as a guide to colour, finish off the outside edge by slip stitching.

3 Cut a 7.5cm (3in) circle of self-adhesive felt. Peel off the protective paper and stick the felt to the back of the work so that it conceals the ends.

4 Fold the ribbon in half and stitch to the edge of the disc. Knot the ends together and trim.

Cup and Saucer

The familiar domestic image of a floral china tea cup and saucer is captured in this needlepoint design. The main part is worked in tent stitch with a border of cushion (pillow) stitch squares. The background is stitched in two shades of the same colour, graded from dark to light. The distinctive shape of the frame – known as an Oxford frame – gives the finished picture a rural aspect and charm.

MATERIALS

20 x 25cm (8 x 10in) piece of 12-count single-thread canvas
Waterproof felt-tip pen
Tapestry needle
1 skein Persian yarn each in dark and light olive, dark and light rust, dark and light pink, light gold, turquoise, dark blue and cream

1 Trace the cup and saucer template directly on to the canvas, using a waterproof felt-tip pen with a fine point. Work the main outline in dark blue tent stitch. Stitch a line of turquoise as a drop shadow.

2 Work the border around the rim and the flowers in pink, the leaves in olive and turquoise, the flower centres in gold and the cup in cream. With two shades of rust, fill in the background rectangle in tent stitch.

3 Next, work three rounds of cushion (pillow) stitch over four threads as a border, using olive for the final round. Stretch and block the finished piece, then fold under the surplus canvas and press.

Sun Pincushion

The sunburst is a universal image of life and energy. Like the heart, it appears as a decorative motif in various forms throughout the world. This interpretation is based on a drawing from a Renaissance manuscript and is worked in three rich golden shades of Persian yarn, with a contrasting cobalt blue background. Basic tent stitch is used throughout, and the finished design is framed with three bands of long-arm cross stitch.

MATERIALS

20cm (8in) square of 10-count double-thread canvas
Masking tape; tacking (basting) thread
Waterproof felt-tip pen; tapestry needle
1 skein Persian yarn each in pale yellow, dark golden
  yellow, warm gold, mid blue, chocolate brown
  and white
Matching cotton sewing thread
41 x 90cm (16 x 36in) piece of polyester wadding
  (batting)
Dressmaker's pins; matching fabric for the backing

1 Bind the edges of the canvas with masking tape to prevent them fraying and mark the centre with two lines of tacking stitch. Trace the design or draw it directly on to the canvas. Use two strands of yarn in the needle throughout. Outline the face first in brown, then pick out the cheeks, eyes, nose and mouth details using the photograph as a guide to colours.

2 Fill in the circle surrounding the face in blue, with rays of pale yellow and warm gold, then complete the square in white. Next, stitch three lines of long-arm cross stitch, using progressive shades of pale yellow, dark golden yellow, then warm gold, to frame the sun. Stretch and block the finished work.

3 Make a pad to fill the cushion (pillow): cut two 15cm (6in), four 12.5cm (5in) and three 10cm (4in) squares of wadding (batting) and stack them as shown. Pin, then stitch together.

4 Cut an 18cm (7in) square of backing fabric and, right sides together, pin and stitch to the needlepoint on three sides. Turn under the 12mm (½in) seam allowance on the fourth side, insert the pad and slip stitch the side closed.

Brooch Cushion (Pillow)

A brooch cushion (pillow) can look very attractive, set among ornaments and cosmetic jars on the dressing table, and it is a good way to display a selection of favourite jewellery. The toning blues of this frilled version have been picked to match the fabric ruffle, but the colour scheme could easily be adapted to coordinate with the furnishings of a particular room.

MATERIALS
25cm (10in) square of 12-count single-thread canvas
Masking tape; tacking (basting) thread
Tapestry yarn:
 2 skeins each in white, pale blue and mid blue
 1 skein each in dark blue and indigo
50 x 75cm (20 x 30in) piece of polyester wadding
 (batting); tapestry needle; dressmaker's pins;
 matching cotton sewing thread
20cm (8in) square of printed fabric for the backing
20 x 122cm (4 x 48in) printed fabric for the frill
Sewing machine

1 Bind the edges of the canvas with masking tape and mark the centre with two lines of contrasting tacking stitch. The checked pattern is worked in diagonal stitch throughout. Start off in the middle of the canvas by working a small square over two threads, using indigo wool. Work a narrow line of mid blue on each side of the square and fill in the corners with white squares.

2 Following the chart, continue to work the checked pattern until the stitched area measures 14.5cm (5¾in). All the stitches should be worked so that they face the same direction, which will mean that the finished piece becomes distorted. Stretch and block it back into a square shape.

3 Make a cushion (pillow) pad by cutting four 16.5cm (6½in), four 14cm (5½in) and four 11.5cm (4in) squares of wadding (batting) and sandwiching them together as shown. Pin around the edge, sew, then trim away the excess. Cut a 16.5cm (6½in) square of backing fabric and, with right sides together, sew to the needlepoint around three sides, sewing close to the stitches. Turn through, clip the corners and press. Insert the cushion (pillow) pad and slip stitch the fourth side closed.

4 Join the short edges of the frill with a French seam, then make a narrow hem all around each long side, turning the fabric over twice to conceal the raw edges.

5 Run a strong gathering thread around one side. Fold the frill into four to mark it into quarters, then pin around the four sides of the cushion (pillow).

6 Draw up the thread and adjust the gathers so that they are even, allowing an extra fullness at the corners. Stitch on to the cushion (pillow) using small neat stitches, and working from the right side.

85

Needle Book and Scissor Case

A holder for needles is essential for everybody who sews, and this ivy-leaf needle book, with its matching scissor case, would make an appropriate gift for an embroiderer. Both are trimmed with cord, and the scissor case has a long loop so that it can be kept within easy reach when working. The symmetrical shape of the dark green leaves is offset by the trailing coils of couched gold thread. The informality of this naturalistic design means that there is no need to be too rigid in placing the leaves or copying the stem lines.

NEEDLE BOOK MATERIALS
Ruler; waterproof felt-tip pen
20 x 25cm (8 x 10in) piece of 12-count single thread
*   canvas; tapestry needle*
Gold metallic thread for the stems
1 skein of tapestry yarn in dark green and 6 skeins in
*   light green; matching cotton sewing thread*
12.5 x 18cm (5 x 7in) piece of green lining fabric
25cm (10in) square of felt; 70cm (28in) length of cord

1 Using a waterproof felt-tip pen, rule a rectangle of 10 x 15cm (4 x 6in) on to the canvas. Trace the design. Stitch the leaves in dark green straight stitch. Fill in the background with light green tent stitch worked on the diagonal from the top right-hand corner. Couch a double strand of gold thread for the stems and tendrils.

2 Press the finished piece lightly, then cut out, adding 12mm (½in) canvas all round. Finger-press turnings to the wrong side. Cut the lining to the same size as the canvas. Press under the 12mm (½in) seam allowance, mitring the corners. Slip stitch to the back of the canvas and press from the wrong side on to a padded surface.

3 Cut four felt pages, slightly smaller than half the finished cover size, and stitch to the back cover.

4 Slip stitch cord around the outer edge of the cover, starting and finishing at the centre top. Knot the ends into a loop.

1 Following the diagram, draw the case outline on to the canvas. Work the four leaves in dark green straight stitch. Fill in the background in tent stitch in light green and couch a double strand of gold thread for the stems and tendrils. Make two pieces, reversing the design for the back.

SCISSOR CASE MATERIALS
Waterproof felt-tip pen
20 x 25cm (8 x10in) piece of 12-count single-thread canvas; tapestry needle
1 skein of tapestry yarn in dark green and 5 skeins in light green
Gold metallic thread for the stems
15 x 20cm (6 x 8in) piece of lining fabric
Sewing machine; matching cotton sewing thread; length of cord

2 Cut out one piece, leaving a margin around the stitching, and cut a piece of lining to the same size. With right sides of canvas and lining facing, stitch close to the worked area down one long side and up the other, leaving the top unstitched between points A and A.

3 Trim the surplus fabric around the stitched line as shown and clip the angles. Clip the canvas and trim the lining on the unstitched top edge. Press under the excess on both sides.

4 Gently turn through to the right side, making sure that the corners are crisp. Tidy the turn-in around the top edge and stitch the lining and canvas together. Lay the work face downwards on a soft pad and press. Repeat the lining process for the second side.

5 With the wrong sides together, slip stitch the two sides, leaving the top open between points A. Trim with cord. Attach the cord to one point A, 35cm (14in) from one end. Slip stitch all around the top opening, then down one side and up the other. Join securely at second point A and cut the two long ends to equal lengths. Tie the two ends together in a knot.

Patchwork and Quilting

To create patchwork, small pieces of fabric are sewn together to make items that can range in scale from a tiny pincushion to a bedcover. The joy of this process is that, even when using a traditional pattern and scraps of recycled cloth, each project will be unique. The beauty of each design lies in its combination of shapes and colours; with imagination, almost anything is possible.

Patchwork and Quilting

Patchwork is constructed from shaped pieces of contrasting fabric, which are sewn together in geometric patterns to form a mosaic of cloth. Quilting is the process by which two sheets of fabric, with padding between them, are joined by lines of stitching. The top layer is often made from patchwork and so the two crafts are closely linked.

The word "quilt" comes from *culcita*, the Latin for a stuffed mattress or cushion (pillow); indeed, a thick bedcover, filled with yarn or even straw, was an essential domestic item in the days before effective heating. The earliest quilts were purely functional, but as time passed, they became more ornate.

Right: This nineteenth-century English quilt is made from dressmaker's remnants. The printed trompe-l'oeil fabric border gives the impression of a hexagonal patchwork.

Below: Patchwork looks effective on any scale. This small heart-shaped pincushion is made from fragments of antique cloth saved from an irreparably damaged quilt.

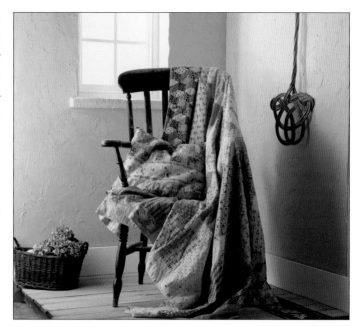

Quilting itself dates back as far as the Middle Ages, when protective padded garments were worn under armour. It was used for insulated doublets, petticoats and nightcaps, as well as for bedcovers. In the past, quilting was practised throughout Europe and was at its most popular in Britain, particularly in Wales and Northumbria. Distinctive wholecloth bedcovers, made from plain red or white woven cotton, were unique to these areas. The flowing quilted designs incorporated spirals, interlocking circles, hearts, feathers, waves and other natural imagery. In west Wales, children were sent out to collect leaves and petals from the hedgerows to use as templates. Making a quilt was part of the daily routine and often a family affair, with even the youngest members threading needles. Women did most of the sewing, and men cut the quilting templates from thin wood or tin.

The early pioneers from Britain and

Contemporary patchwork can be bold and graphic in design, like these velvet cushion (pillow) covers.

bees" were an important social event, usually held before haymaking, when friends and neighbours would gather together at dawn with the object of completing their work before sundown.

Quilters have always been resourceful and open to ideas. The first bedcovers were stitched and quilted by hand, but new techniques were eagerly adopted when domestic sewing machines appeared in the 1870s. Very often the patchwork would be pieced by machine, then the quilting designs worked by hand. This combination is

the Netherlands took basic household linens with them to America, but the comparative scarcity and high cost of cloth encouraged a new economy. Patchwork quilt tops used scraps salvaged from outworn clothing, while old blankets, rags or raw cotton were all used as fillings. In more remote areas, homespun cotton fabric was often used, coloured with the same vegetable dyes that the Native Americans used.

As more printed and patterned fabrics became available, the characteristic pattern blocks developed, based on a combination of squares, triangles and diamonds. Their names are a social document in themselves. They might reflect the makers' religious beliefs, as in "Star of Bethlehem" and "Garden of Eden", or the dangers of frontier

existence: "Bear's Paw", "Rocky Road to Kansas" and "Indian Hatchet". Some were named after individuals, such as "Aunt Sukey's Choice", and "Grandmother's Favourite", while others evoked the objects of everyday life: "Weather Vane", "Monkey Wrench" and "Churn Dash".

Tradition has it that a young woman had to make eleven bedcovers before she married, and that the twelfth was a rich wedding quilt. The pattern chosen for this would often contain visual references to the couple – a fragment of a flag for a soldier, nautical patterns for a sailor or the "Little School House" design for a teacher.

Patchwork tops were generally pieced by just one worker, but quilting was a community effort, with several women sewing around the frame. "Quilting

Pieces cut from furnishing fabrics and an embroidered traycloth have been combined to make this brightly coloured floral panel.

still used, but machine quilting is increasingly popular because it is so quick. Lightweight polyester waddings (battings) have superseded the old fillings and these can easily be quilted by machine. Specialist suppliers now stock the materials needed to make professionally finished quilts and new ways of transferring designs and shaped pieces have been introduced. Interest in these adaptable and creative needlecrafts is widespread and growing – they are a developing art and a living tradition.

Album quilts can be made as a group project, with each contributor making one block, or as a showcase for the many named traditional patterns.

Patchwork and Quilting
Tools and Materials

O nly the most basic needlework tools are needed to start patchwork and quilting, although a range of equipment is now available to make precision cutting and assembly both easier and quicker. A sewing machine is useful for piecing techniques and a good steam iron is needed to prepare fabric and press seams.

FABRIC
The various materials used in a single project should all be of the same weight; medium-weight homespun checks, dressmaking cottons or lawn with small-scale designs are ideal, but should be washed before use to pre-shrink and remove any excess dye. Specialist mail-order companies stock a wide range of patchwork fabrics in both prints and complementary plain colours. Wadding (batting) for quilting is produced in both iron-on and sew-in variations in several weights. The old cotton type is still used today.

THREADS
Ordinary sewing thread is used for machine piecing and can be strengthened by running it over beeswax when quilting or hand sewing. Extra-strong quilting thread is available in a variety of colours.

TOOLS AND ACCESSORIES
Transparent rulers and square measures can be used to draw up templates or in conjunction with a rotary cutter to produce accurate fabric shapes. A cutting board will protect the work surface from the sharp blade of the cutter. Dressmaker's shears should have sharp blades and be kept only for cutting fabric; use another pair for paper or card and small embroidery scissors for cutting threads. Ready-made templates come in geometric shapes with clear plastic windows. Dressmaker's chalk or special quilter's pencils can be used to mark seam allowances or quilting patterns on to fabric and fine rust-proof dressmaker's pins are used to hold the pieces together. Short quilter's needles are best for hand quilting and a metal thimble provides very necessary protection. Special quilter's thimbles and finger guards are also produced.

Quilting threads.

Sewing cotton.

Thimble.

Rotary cutter.

Beeswax.

Quilter's needles.

Small sharp scissors.

Quilting hoop.

Homespun checks and stripes.

Plain cottons.

Templates.

Floral prints.

Dressmaker's pencils.

Transparent grid ruler.

Quilters square measure, with wadding (batting) on top.

93

Cutting Out and Piecing

There are three ways of piecing or joining patchwork pieces: by machine, by hand or with backing papers. Machining is quickest, but hand sewing gives a traditional, slightly irregular seam. For the beginner, working over backing papers is the best way to make precise diamonds and other angled shapes. Whichever method is chosen, meticulous measurement and cutting, careful stitching and thorough pressing are all vital for a professional finish.

Right: The checkerboard centre of this cushion (pillow) cover was cut from striped seersucker and remnants of floral furnishing fabric.

1 USING A ROTARY CUTTER
Working on a cutting mat, match one corner of the measure to the grain of the fabric. Keeping the cutter upright, run it firmly along the measure, and cut along the two sides.

2 Turn the measure and line up the markings with the two cut edges to form the size of square required. Cut around the other two sides.

3 Squares can be cut in half diagonally to form triangles. Strips and rectangles can be cut using a transparent ruler marked with a grid.

1 MACHINE PIECING SQUARES Set the machine to straight stitch and adjust to 10 stitches every 2.5cm (1in). Pin or hold two squares together, right sides facing and sew along one edge. Leave a seam allowance of 6mm (¼in), using the lines on the machine bed as a guide. Several pairs can be sewn in a continuous line, then cut apart.

2 Join the pairs into strips, then press the seam allowances to one side. Sew the strips together, matching the joins, so that the allowances lie in opposite directions.

1 HAND PIECING
To be sure of a neat seam, the allowance – usually 6mm (¼in) – is marked on the back of the fabric. With window templates, the metal shape can be used as a guide, or rule a line with a quilter's pencil or fading pen.

2 Cut a length of sewing thread, about 45cm (18in) long, and strengthen by pulling it against a beeswax block. Knot the end, then, holding the two pieces right sides together, make a line of small tidy running stitches along the edge. Finish with a back stitch.

1 WORKING WITH BACKING PAPERS Special templates with a transparent plastic window are useful when using patterned fabrics, but they must be lined up with the grain. The dark edge represents the seam allowance.

2 Use the metal shape as a guide for cutting the backing paper. Pin or tack (baste) it to the centre of the fabric shape, then fold the seam allowance over the paper and tack (baste) down, one side at a time.

3 When working over sharp angles, the surplus fabric can be mitred to a neat point and tacked (basted) down. The pieces are joined together with over-stitching (see method for hexagons); the tacking (basting) stitch and papers are then removed.

This mosaic is based on a tile design from the Alhambra in Spain. The interlocking shapes were worked over papers to achieve a flat and accurate pattern.

Storm at Sea

This stunning pattern originated on the eastern seaboard of the United States. The overall effect is one of lively flowing movement, suggesting ocean waves, but all the seams are, in fact, straight. Although complex at first sight, the patchwork is made up of just three different blocks: the large pale blue square is bordered on each side by a blue diamond block, with small dark blue squares at each corner. The method for making these is also a general guide to machine piecing techniques for triangles. To construct the actual pattern, draw up a set of templates on squared paper using the finished picture as a guide.

1 The large and small square blocks are pieced in the same way. Sew a white triangle to each side of the smallest square, stitching 6mm (¼in) from the edge. Press the seams so that the allowance faces inwards.

2 Sew a blue triangle along each edge of the square, carefully pinning to match the seams. It may be helpful to tack (baste) the pieces together first.

3 The large square blocks are pieced in the same order. Press the allowance out towards the corners. This prevents the fabric showing through the white cotton.

4 The diamond-shaped blocks are constructed from two squares, each consisting of a dark triangle with a narrow white triangle stitched to two sides.

5 Lay the completed blocks out in rows and stitch together. Careful pinning and tacking (basting) is necessary when working with such large pieces, to keep the seams and joins regular.

Bear's Paw

Bear's paw or bear's track is an early American pattern, supposedly inspired by pawprints left in the mud. It is a repeating design with the square blocks joined with bands of fabric or sashing. In the past, a patchwork quilt top was worked in one piece, then quilted on a large frame, but today there is not always time or room to do this. Instead, the blocks can be quilted individually, then joined.

Above: This bear's paw quilt has been made entirely from recycled fabric such as old gingham shirts and white sheeting.

1 Each block is made up of four "paws" surrounding a small square and with a row of three white squares between them. Follow the main picture to assemble the block.

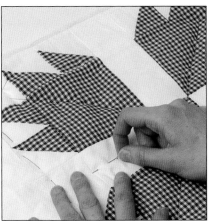

2 Cut pieces of backing fabric and wadding (batting) slightly larger than the finished block and tack (baste) together, working from the centre out. Be sure that the layers lie flat. Quilt along the seam lines.
To join the completed blocks, stitch them together in strips, divided by bands of single white squares.

3 When joining the blocks, sew through the top layer only and press seam flat. Trim the excess wadding (batting) so the edges just touch. Sew the wadding with a loose flat stitch.

4 To neaten the back seams, fold and sew each seam so it overlaps onto the next square. Slip stitch then complete the quilting along the remaining seam lines.

Hexagonal Patchwork

Unlike block designs, which may consist of many different-shaped pieces, hexagonal patchwork uses just one shape. The pattern is formed by the choice and arrangement of colours within the honeycomb grid made by the interlocking repeat. Hexagons are traditionally worked over backing papers, which should be firm enough to hold their shape but not so thick that they are difficult to sew through. A quicker way of piecing is to use a lightweight washable interfacing. This remains inside the patches, giving them extra support.

Above: Silks and velvets were used to make this antique-effect cushion (pillow) cover; the use of a black outline around the rosettes is particularly dramatic.

1 JOINING HEXAGONS
Use a template as a guide for cutting papers or, if interfacing is being used, draw on to it directly with a sharp pencil, then cut out.

2 Iron the interfacing to the wrong side of the fabric following the manufacturer's instructions and keeping the shapes parallel to the grain. Cut out, leaving a margin of at least 6mm (¼in) all around.

3 Turn the seam allowance back over the iron-on interfacing. Take care not to crease the hexagon. Finally, tack (baste) down all around using small stitches.

4 The patches are joined with a neat stitch, which should pass through the fabric without picking up any of the interfacing. Hold the pieces together with right sides facing.

5 Six coloured patches can be sewn around a contrasting centre to make a rosette. These are then joined to make an all-over pattern. Take out the tacking (basting) when the work is complete.

Patchwork Gallery

The heritage of patchwork patterns is enormous; there are literally hundreds of named designs and variations from which to choose, and all quiltmakers bring their own individual interpretation to their work.

Geometric patterns, sometimes from surprising sources, can be adapted – the scope is limitless. The selection on this page illustrates what is possible, both for the beginner and for the more experienced worker.

Left: "Basket of scraps" consists of four patterned diamonds set on a triangle. It makes a good showcase for different floral prints. The blocks could also be set in rows all facing the same way.

Left: "Ships in harbour" shows how a complicated pattern can be built up by repeating a simple square block. Study the design carefully to see how this is done.

Above: "Dresden plate" originated in the United States in the 1920s. It is a combination of appliquéd and patchwork techniques which looks most effective when fabrics of a similar pattern density are used together.

Left: This abstract patchwork is made up from randomly arranged plain and patterned squares and uses fragments of hand-dyed cotton and satin.

Above: A drawing of a Roman pavement was the basis for this example, which is made up of squares and long hexagonal shapes. The use of a strong plain colour against a subtly patterned background gives depth to the design.

Left: This intricate *trompe-l'oeil* design, a variation of "tumbling blocks", was worked over backing papers. The basic unit is a 3-D hexagon surrounded by nine diamonds.

Crazy Patchwork

There was a great vogue for this highly ornamental patchwork in the late nineteenth century; it appealed to the Victorians' desire for lavish interior decoration and their love of thrift, as even the smallest and most irregular scraps of fabric can be incorporated. It is worked in individual squares which can be used singly, or joined to make a throw or quilt.

1 Collect together remnants of silk, velvet, brocade and furnishing fabric. Cut out and arrange random pieces of material into a square, then cut a square of calico (cotton lining fabric) to use as the foundation.

2 The patches can be hand sewn on to the calico (lining fabric) with running stitch, or machined with a matching or contrasting decorative stitch. Work from one edge across the square, attaching one piece at a time.

3 Embroidered or appliquéd motifs can be added for a luxurious effect.

Above: This fringed cushion (pillow) incorporates fragments of Indian woven braid with silk salvaged from old ties. It has been embroidered with a variety of elaborate stitches.

4 Further decoration can be added by disguising the seams with embroidery stitches worked in bright colours. Feather stitch and its variations are especially popular.

Somerset Patchwork

Somerset and crazy patchwork both involve stitching individual pieces of material on to a foundation fabric, instead of piecing them together. Neither technique is really suitable for items that will get a lot of wear and tear, but both are attractive and intriguing to construct. For the best result, choose strong, contrasting colours to form the folded star design. Dressmaking-weight cottons will give a crisp edge and are not too bulky, as the finished piece is made up of many layers.

1 Each triangle is made from a rectangle, with its length twice the width, plus 6mm (¼in) seam allowance at one long edge. Press under the turning, then fold the neatened edges over to make a right-angled triangle.

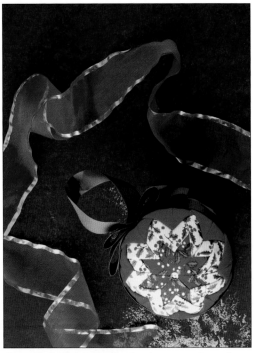

Above: Craft fabric in small-scale prints was used to make this festive Christmas decoration.

2 Cut a square of firm cotton. Fold and press diagonally each way from corner to corner, then in half vertically and horizontally. Arrange the first four triangles as shown, and sew in place along the outer edges. Sew each point with a small invisible stitch.

4 Continue to build up the pattern in contrasting rounds, making sure that each layer overlaps the previous one.

3 The next eight triangles are arranged to match up with the guides, so that a star shape is created. Measure each piece before stitching, so that they are all equidistant.

WORKING IN THE ROUND This technique can also be worked over a large polystyrene ball. Work in two halves, pin the triangles in place and cover the join with a ribbon.

Suffolk Puffs (Yo-yo Patchwork)

S uffolk puff, also known as yo-yo patchwork,
has a charming flower-like appearance. It is
quick to assemble from gathered circles of fabric,
which can be lightly padded to give extra depth.
Different patterns can be created by arranging the
yo-yos in stripes or concentric circles. The finished
piece drapes well and makes an attractive bedcover,
especially if placed over a coloured blanket which
shows through the gaps. Alternatively, it can be
made more hardwearing by backing with a
contrasting fabric.

Above: The circles can be joined in rows, as shown in the
steps, but a denser effect can be achieved by setting them in
a honeycomb arrangement to form hexagonal shapes.

1 Cut a circle of card measuring between 7.5cm (3in) and
15cm (6in), or use a suitable saucer as a template. With
this as a guide, cut out the patches, grouping them according
to colour. Light cotton fabrics, fine enough to gather
without being bulky, are best.

3 Carefully pull up the thread and distribute the folds
evenly. Be sure that all the raw edges lie on the inside.
Secure with a few back stitches and trim the thread.

2 Turn under a narrow hem to the wrong side of the fabric
around the edge of the circle. Stitch down with small
running stitches, using a strong thread.

4 When all the circles have been prepared, sort them
into groups of colour and lay them out on the finished
design. Join the edges where they touch with several strong
stitches, without distorting the shape.

Cathedral Window

C athedral window, like Suffolk puff (yo-yo patchwork), is a fascinating technique which does not need to be lined or quilted. The distinctive lattice is formed by joining folded squares of plain fabric to frame small patches of patterned material. It is important to cut and stitch accurately to achieve a uniform result.

1 Cut a square of cotton or calico twice the size of the finished square, plus a hem of 6mm (¼in). Press under the allowance along each side.

Above: This dramatic example uses metallic fabrics to give a jewel-like effect. It combines Cathedral Window patchwork with a variation known as Secret Garden.

2 Fold the four corners to the middle of the square so that the points meet exactly and press. Pin in place.

3 Fold the double thickness corners to the centre, press the creases and pin in place. Sew the four points firmly and neatly together with a matching thread.

4 Sew the cotton squares together, right sides facing, to form a block. The coloured patches are fixed on to the diamonds created between the sewn-together squares.

5 Cut a square of fabric 6mm (¼ in) smaller than the diamond and pin in place. Fold the sides of the four surrounding squares back over the raw edges of the fabric and stitch down. Triangles can be used to fill in the spaces at the sides.

Hand and Machine Quilting

Quilting simply involves working lines of hand or machine stitching to hold a padded filling between two pieces of fabric. The stitches pass through all three layers. It is often used to enhance a piece of patchwork, but is also an independent technique; designs worked on to plain fabrics are known as wholecloth motifs. There are many traditional variations, often based on natural imagery. Quilting patterns can be transferred by the methods used for embroidery, but cardboard templates are often used for repeated shapes.

1 HAND QUILTING
Place the template on to the fabric and draw round the edge with a dressmaker's fading pen.

Above: Quilting stitches can be used in a free and illustrative way. This padded cherub was painted on to silk and outlined with back stitch.

2 Use a graded measure to rule the parallel lines that form the characteristic grid pattern. Be sure that they are set at right angles.

4 Using strong quilting thread, sew over the outline with a small running stitch. To avoid the knot showing on the back, tug the thread so that it is pulled through the fabric into the wadding (batting). Pick up three or four stitches at a time and stitch with an even motion.

3 Sandwich the wadding (batting) between the top cloth and a piece of backing fabric. Tack (baste) together diagonally and around the outside edge, so that the surface lies smoothly.

5 Do not carry loose threads across the back of the work, but sew each line of the design separately by passing the needle through the quilt. Finish off with a back stitch.

QUILTING ON PATCHWORK As well as serving the practical purpose of anchoring the wadding (batting), quilting can add depth and texture to a piece of patchwork. Here *(left)* it has been used to emphasize the eight diamonds that make up the "birds-in-the-air" design.

A line of stitching is worked either side of each seam.

TRANSFER TO DARK FABRICS Regular motifs such as this flower can be drawn using a template from which one repeating petal has been cut out. Draw round the outline first, then move the template one step at a time and mark the curved lines.

Above: Quilting designs can be worked in light thread on a dark background for a strong visual contrast. A quilter's silver pencil will show up well and gives a fine line.

MACHINE QUILTING Quilting by machine gives a very regular appearance to the finished piece and is quick to do. Some sewing machines have special quilting attachments which are helpful when sewing in parallel rows. Be sure that the tension is adjusted correctly before starting and stitch slowly at a regular pace.

The layers must be well tacked (basted) so that they do not shift. Use a thread to match the fabric and stitch as close to the seam as possible. Both hands should guide the work under the presser foot.

Quilting Gallery

O ver the years, quilting has been used to produce many decorative effects, in conjunction with patchwork or on its own. This collection of old and new examples shows just what can be achieved and should provide a great source of inspiration.

Above: The rows of stitching that quilt these antique bedcovers had to be worked closely to hold in place the rather unstable cotton filling.

Above: The hearts and interlaced knots on this machine-stitched wedding quilt are symbols of love and betrothal. It is a beautiful example of how a traditional design can be interpreted in a contemporary way.

Left: The handle of the green basket has been "echo" quilted, with the shape repeated in concentric lines, while the overlapping strips that make up the pineapple motif have been simply outlined.

Left: Instead of outlining the patchwork pieces, the maker of this turkey red bear's paw motif has quilted it with a grid of white stitching, worked across the entire surface.

Below: These entertaining hearts are made from padded and quilted velvet and trimmed with fake fur.

Above: Outline stitching has been used to define just the white triangles of this floral patchwork border. New types of polyester waddings (battings) do not have to be stitched as densely as the old cotton fillings.

3-Dimensional Quilting

PADDED QUILTING

A quick and effective way of giving a quilted look to a printed fabric is to pad individual motifs. This works well on floral chintzes and can be used for soft furnishings, to give interest to cushions (pillows) or headboards.

1 Tack (baste) the printed fabric together with a piece of thick wadding (batting) and a cotton backing cloth. Be sure the layers all lie flat.

2 Pick out a few flowers that are evenly spaced across the surface and sew around them, through all three layers, with either a straight or satin stitch, following the outline closely.

3 When complete, turn over and cut away the excess wadding (batting) between the stitched areas. For extra depth, make a slit in the backing fabric, stuff in a small amount of wadding (batting) and stitch back together.

CORD QUILTING Interlaced patterns such as this Celtic knot can be created by threading a soft yarn or cord through a stitched channel. The shadow effect is created by using a sheer fabric for the top layer so that the green yarn shows through.

Outline the design with two evenly spaced rows of back stitch *(left)*. Working from the back, thread a tapestry needle with cord and insert between the lines of stitching. Bring the needle out and back to get round the curves, leaving a small loop so that it does not pull *(right)*.

TRAPUNTO QUILTING This complex design was worked by tacking (basting) two layers of fabric together and outlining the design with back stitch. Single shapes were then stuffed with wadding (batting), as above. This padded technique can be used with cord quilting to create interesting effects.

Checked Cushion (Pillow)

This checked cushion (pillow) is a unique mixture of the old and new. The green and red gingham cloth has been taken from outworn garments, while the antique engravings have been transferred on to cotton material, using a newly developed technique. Image transfer is an exciting medium, by which any photocopied picture can be fixed on to fabric, and its possibilities are endless.

MATERIALS
Image-transfer (photo transfer) solution
Illustrations of fruit and vegetables
Scraps of checked and gingham fabric
White cotton fabric
Cushion (pillow) pad
Sewing thread; decorative buttons

1 Photocopy your chosen engravings, enlarging the scale if necessary, and cut out. Use special image-copying solution to transfer the photocopies on to plain white cotton fabric, following the manufacturer's instructions.

2 Collect together a selection of toning checked fabrics and scraps, and cut them into rectangular shapes. Cut the transferred images to size and sort the various patches into a pleasing arrangement that fits the size of the cushion (pillow) pad.

3 Sew the patches together, starting with the shortest edges first and pressing all the seams open. Sew on the buttons for a decorative finish. Cut a piece of fabric 12mm (½in) larger all round than the cushion pad and, with right sides facing, pin to the patchwork piece. Sew together around three sides and clip the corners. Turn through and press lightly, then insert the cushion (pillow) pad and slip stitch the fourth side closed.

Red Star

The bold combination of turkey red and plain white was a favourite colour scheme among nineteenth-century American quilters. This project continues the thrifty tradition of early patchwork, using re-cycled cotton sheeting which has been dyed in two different shades of dark red. The variation in colour adds a dynamic quality to the surface of the quilt. It is worked in the English style, using backing papers, but the patches could equally be sewn together by machine. The finished piece measures 70cm (28in) square.

MATERIALS
Old white cotton bed sheet
Hot-water dye in scarlet and crimson
Thick paper for cutting the templates
Tracing paper
Tacking thread
Cotton sewing thread
Beeswax; dressmaker's pins
75cm (30in) square of iron-on quilting

1 Discard any worn areas of the sheet. Following the manufacturer's instructions, dye half of the fabric in two shades of red. Trace the inner diamond template accurately and use it to cut out 72 backing papers. From the cotton cut 40 red and 32 white diamonds, using the outer template as a guide. Tack a fabric diamond to each paper one, folding over the surplus fabric at the points.

2 Overstitch the edges of the diamonds together with right sides facing. Pull the sewing thread over a block of beeswax to prevent it fraying. Assemble eight large diamonds, following the finished picture.

3 Join the eight diamonds together to form a star, making sure that the centre points all butt together tidily. Press from the right side, then remove the papers.

4 Cut a 54cm (21in) square of white cotton. From red cotton, cut four 12.5 x 54cm (5 x 21in) strips and four 12.5cm (5in) squares. Sew two of the strips to opposite sides of the main square, leaving a 12mm (½in) seam allowance. Join a red square to each end of the other two strips and sew in place to complete the border. Pin the star to the centre of the white square.

5 Slip stitch the star in place, tucking under any surplus fabric. Cut the iron-on quilting into a square measuring 12mm (½in) less than the panel and fix to the reverse side. Back with cotton and tidy up the edges.

Saw-Tooth Star Bag

The saw-tooth star pattern, like many other patchwork patterns, derives its name from the simple surroundings of everyday life: the triangular shapes around the four sides suggest the sharp teeth of a saw blade. The star, an old variation of the basic four-square block, is ideally suited to the homespun cotton checks which make this useful drawstring bag.

MATERIALS
Tracing paper
Pencil
Remnants of 3 different checked fabrics
Matching cotton sewing thread
Safety pin
Dressmaker's pins
Potpourri or lavender flowers

1 Enlarge and trace the templates, which include a seam allowance. Cut one large square from the darkest fabric, four small squares and four large triangles from the mid-tone, and eight small triangles from the lightest check.

2 Join the small and large triangles together, piecing by hand or machine. Press the seam allowance to one side, away from the large triangle. Pin one block to each of two opposite sides of the main square, then stitch. Press the seams outwards.

3 Take the small squares of mid-tone fabric and join one to each end of the other two blocks. Pin these to the main piece, along the long edges. Stitch the seams, then press so that they lie facing away from the centre square.

4 Cut two rectangles of 16.5 x 27cm (6½ x 10½in) and 16.5 x 42cm (6½ x 16½in) from the mid-tone fabric. Sew the smaller piece to one side of the square, and the longer piece to the opposite edge, allowing for a 6mm (¼in) seam. Fold in half, right sides together, and join the side seams. Turn through, fold top in half, turn in and hem.

5 Sew a 2.5cm (1in) wide drawstring channel, 2.5cm (1in) down from the top edge. Take out the side seam between the two rows of stitching on the right-hand side. Cut a length of matching fabric measuring 5 x 60cm (2 x 24in). Sew it together lengthways, 12mm (½in) away from the raw edges.

6 Trim the seam allowance on the matching fabric and fasten a safety pin to one end. Feed this back inside the tube and turn the drawstring through. Press, then thread through the channel, tying the ends in a knot. Fill the bag with potpourri or lavender flowers.

Log-Cabin Yarn Roll

A full-sized cover in log-cabin patchwork would provide a colourful and dramatic focal point in any bedroom. Undertaking a large-scale quilt, however, is a real labour of love which can take many months, if not years. This yarn holder, which is made from three log-cabin blocks, is a perfect compromise for those whose time is limited. It is a good way to learn how the design is assembled and how its visual impact relies on the contrast between light and dark fabrics.

MATERIALS
Fabric marker pen; dressmaker's pins
20 x 56cm (8 x 22in) piece of calico or other cotton fabric
Selection of cotton fabric pieces sorted into dark and light patterns
20 x 51cm (8 x 20in) piece of patterned fabric for the lining
Sewing machine; matching cotton sewing thread
1.37m (1½yd) length of 12mm (½in) ribbon

1 For each of the three blocks, cut an 18cm (7in) square from plain fabric. Draw two diagonal lines across the square to mark the centre and to help position the strips. Cut a 4.5cm (1¾in) square of plain-coloured fabric and tack (baste) to the centre of the square. Cut 3cm (1¼in) strips of fabric for the four rounds that will surround the square, using the template as a guide, enlarging if necessary.

2 Place the first light strip, pattern side down, along the top edge of the central square. Lower the feed dog on the machine and stitch down along the outside edge. Fold back and press flat. Working clockwise, sew on the second light strip in the same way, then the two dark strips.

3 Continue stitching the strips down in rounds, keeping the dark and light colours on opposite sides, and overlapping each round to allow a 6mm (¼in) seam.

4 Sew the three blocks together in a row and press the seams open. Cut a rectangle of lining fabric which is the same width as, and slightly longer than, the strip. With right sides together, pin and sew along the two long sides and one short end, clip the corners, turn through and press. Fold the overlapping end tidily over the patchwork, pin and slip stitch down.

5 Sew a length of ribbon to the outside of the roll to form a tie.

Crazy Quilt

The random patterning of crazy patchwork makes it quick and enjoyable to work; it does not require a great deal of pre-planning or accurate measurement. This small quilt – which would make a good play mat for a baby – is made from an assortment of striped cotton fabrics. The raw edges are concealed with lines of dark red feather-stitching, which contrasts with the pastel blues and pinks of the shirting. The finished quilt measures 60cm (24in) square.

MATERIALS
Scraps of striped cotton shirting and chambray
Dressmaker's pins
Cotton sewing thread
Stranded embroidery thread in dark red
70cm (28in) square of lightweight iron-on wadding (batting)
70cm (28in) square of backing fabric

1 Cut a 20cm (8in) square of plain fabric. From the striped cottons cut out irregular strips and shapes, then lay them out on the foundation square, in an interesting pattern.

2 Pin the pattern in place and sew down with running stitch. Sew the outer edges, then with three strands of dark red thread, work lines of feather stitching over the joins.

3 Make a further eight blocks, then join them in three rows of three. Sew the three strips together and press the seams open.

4 Cut the iron-on wadding (batting) to the same size as the patchwork and, following the manufacturer's instructions, iron it on to the reverse side.

5 From the backing fabric cut a square that measures 5cm (2in) greater than the quilt. Press under 12mm (½in) all round, then pin to the back of the quilt. Fold the tidied edge over to the right side and slip stitch securely down, mitring the corners.

Linen Throw

I n the past, the care of domestic linen – pillow cases, sheets, napkins, table cloths and runners – was an essential part of household management, and in the wealthiest homes special maids were employed to look after the laundry. Many mats, cloths and covers have survived, but they are not always practical for ordinary use. This all-white quilt is made up of squares cut from old linen, and uses the most interesting types of insertion, embroidery, monograms and pintucking.

MATERIALS
Assortment of old household textiles
Fabric marker pen (washable)
Thin cardboard; dressmaker's pins
White cotton sewing thread
Traditional cotton batting or polyester wadding
Old bed sheet
Contrasting cotton sewing thread
Thick white crochet cotton
Large-eyed sharp needle

1 The quilt can be made to any size, depending on the amount of fabric available. Cut a 20cm (8in) square from thin cardboard to use as a template. Selecting the best textures and patterns, draw around the template on to the fabric and cut a series of patches.

2 Spread the squares out and arrange in regular rows. Using white cotton, sew in pairs, pressing the seams open. Then join into blocks of four and sew the blocks together until the whole quilt top has been pieced together.

3 Cut a piece of batting or wadding the same size as the patchwork, joining if necessary. Use an old bed sheet to back the work, and tack (baste) three layers together with a contrasting thread. Trim back the wadding and the backing layer so that they measure 2cm (¾in) less than the quilt.

4 Thread a large-eyed needle with crochet cotton and back stitch through all three layers at one-corner intersection. Tie the ends tightly with a reef or weaver's knot and trim to 12mm (½in). Repeat over the whole surface.

5 Turn under a 12mm (½in) hem all around the quilt top and fold the surplus over to the wrong side. Slip stitch to the backing fabric, mitring the corners.

Chair Seat

Two different colourways of the same floral furnishing chintz are used for this padded chair seat, giving a chequerboard (checkerboard) effect. "Tied quilting", using narrow pink ribbon, holds the layers together, and ribbon bows are used to attach the pad to the chair. The project serves as an introduction to cutting and piecing basic square patches, and shows how to match the seams together for a professional result.

MATERIALS
Rotary cutter; cutting board
Quilter's square
Remnants of floral furnishing fabric
Dressmaker's pins; matching cotton sewing thread
90cm (36in) length of 2.5cm (1in) ribbon
90cm (36in) length of 10mm (⅜in) ribbon
Thick polyester wadding (batting)
Large-eyed sharp needle

1 With the quilter's square and a rotary cutter, cut out eight light and eight dark squares from the floral fabric, each measuring 10cm (4in). Hold the cutter upright on the cutting board, and always move it away from the body, as the blade is very sharp.

2 Lay the squares out in four rows of four, alternating the colourways, in a pleasing pattern. Join them together in rows of four, stitching 12mm (½in) in from the edge. Press the seams open. Pin the rows together, carefully aligning the seams. Sew together, leaving an identical seam allowance.

3 When the whole square has been completed, press the seams open. As backing, cut a piece of coordinating fabric to the same size as the seat top. Then, with right sides together, pin the cover to the backing fabric.

4 Cut the 2.5cm (1in) wide length of ribbon in two and fold each piece in half. With the fold outermost, sandwich the ribbons between the layers, and pin in place 2.5cm (1in) in from either edge of one side.

5 Sew around three sides of the square and turn through. Cut three layers of wadding (batting) the same size as the seat cover and tack (baste) together. Place inside the cover and slip stitch the fourth side closed.

6 Thread a large-eyed needle with the thin ribbon and push through the seat cover, close to the corner of one square. Bring up to the right side, on the other side of the intersection, and tie the ends in a tight reef knot. Clip back to 2cm (¾in) and repeat across the whole seat cover.

Heart Cushion (Pillow)

This romantic lacy cushion (pillow) would be equally suitable as a present for a bride, or as a valentine gift. The design of interlocked hearts is machine-quilted on to raw silk, and emphasized with the addition of tiny seed-pearl beads. The edge is finished with a ruffle of antique lace. It could be made as a precious keepsake, using remnants of fabric and trimmings left from a wedding dress, and used as a ring cushion (pillow).

MATERIALS
Tracing paper; pencil; thin cardboard; ruler
15 x 35cm (6 x 14in) piece of cream silk
Dressmaker's fading pen; dressmaker's pins
18 x 20cm (7 x 8in) piece of polyester
 wadding (batting); 18 x 20cm (7 x 8in)
 piece of white cotton fabric
Sewing machine; matching sewing thread
122cm (48in) length of 5cm (2in) lace
Polyester toy stuffing; tiny seed-pearl beads

1 Trace the heart motif on to thin cardboard and cut out. From the silk fabric cut a 15 x 18cm (6 x 7in) rectangle. Using a dressmaker's fading pen, rule two diagonal lines to mark the centre. Place the template in the middle of the cross and draw round it, then draw a 15mm (⅝ in) grid across the rest of the fabric.

2 Tack (baste) the cushion (pillow) top to the wadding and back with cotton fabric to prevent it snagging in the machine. Thread the machine with matching thread and stitch over the grid and heart outline. (The fading pen lines will disappear in a few hours.) Trim back the excess wadding (batting) and square off the edges.

3 Cut a second piece of silk to the same size, pin to the right side of the quilted piece and stitch together, leaving a space. Clip the corners, turn through, and fill with stuffing. Slip stitch the space closed.

4 Join the ends of the lace and run a line of gathering stitches along the straight edge. Pin to the corners of the cushion (pillow), even out the gathers and over-stitch. Sew seed pearls where quilting lines cross.

Hexagonal Pincushion

The all-over mosaic effect of hexagonal patches is surprisingly easy to achieve, as the shapes do not have any sharp angles to be joined. Six-sided shapes are usually worked over a paper backing, rather than being sewn together with straight stitch, and this way of assembling must be used when working on a small scale. The miniature patchwork technique could be extended to make a tiny quilt for a doll's house.

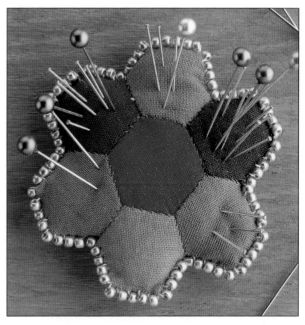

MATERIALS
Isometric graph paper
Ruler; pen; thin cardboard
Scraps of cotton fabric; cotton sewing thread
Small quantity of polyester wadding
  (batting)
Embroidery scissors: rocaille beads

1 Following the triangular grid printed on the isometric graph paper, use a pen and ruler to mark out fourteen hexagons with 10mm (⅜in) sides. Cut out accurately. These are the backing papers.

2 Draw a hexagon on thin cardboard to use as a template for cutting the fabric: it should measure approximately 6mm (¼in) greater all round than the backing paper. Use the template as a guide to cut out the patches. Tack each patch centrally on to a backing paper, then fold over and tack down the seam allowance, making sure that the corners are tidy.

3 Sew the patches together by overstitching the outside edges, picking up just two threads of fabric on each side with each stitch and holding them with right sides facing. Join into two rosettes of seven hexagons each.

4 Press lightly and remove the backing papers. With wrong sides facing, overstitch rosettes together, leaving a small space at one side. Stuff the pincushion with polyester wadding (batting), using the point of a pair of scissors to ease the fibre carefully right into the corners. Oversew the space and then sew rocaille beads around the outside edge to make a decorative border.

Appliqué

Appliqué is the simple process of stitching one fabric on to another. The application of fabrics, however, takes many forms. It can be purely functional or more highly decorative, and ranges from patching a worn knee on a garment to combining specially chosen materials to produce attractive, soft furnishings for the home. The end results can be simply stunning!

Appliqué

Appliqué, or applied work, is the craft of creating a design by sewing cut-out shapes from one material on to a background cloth. Unlike patchwork, where pieces are joined to create a new fabric, appliquéd shapes are added to an existing foundation. Its origins were strictly utilitarian, arising from the need to repair damage, but appliqué has developed into an extravagant art form in itself.

Appliqué is, even so, inextricably linked to patchwork and quilting, and the three techniques often appear together. Cut-out shapes can be more ornamental than pieced work and detailed patterns can be created. Appliqué is often used to add detail to geometric motifs, or to create lavish swags to border a patchwork design.

In eighteenth-century Britain, appliqué was used to conserve fragments of fine fabric, and to produce new bedspreads and wall hangings. New and exotic textiles, such as the Indian tree of life designs, were valued as highly as porcelain and other imported artefacts, so every precious scrap had to be used. Wealthy ladies of leisure, living in grand houses, would cut out the printed motifs and

This bird design, in strong primary colours, comes from the Indian district of Barmer, near Pakistan. It is finished with chain stitch.

reassemble them on to a new backing. Many examples of their work have been preserved in their original locations, valued for the skill involved in making them and for the intrinsic worth of the fabric itself.

Distinctive appliqué techniques have evolved in many areas of the world, as part of the needlework traditions of diverse cultures. In the Indian state of Gujarat, appliqué is used in the home for cushions, bedspreads and door-hangings, while large-scale pattern-cut banners and canopies have ceremonial

significance. The motifs used are bright and bold, so that they have great visual impact in a bustling procession.

The clothing of the tribal people of the north of Thailand is adorned with panels of intricate reverse appliqué. Here colour plays as important a role as patterns, and younger women traditionally wear much brighter and more vibrantly coloured clothing than their elders.

Perhaps the most spectacular appliqué quilts are those originally made in Hawaii. The technique was introduced

Soft pastel cottons, edged with blanket stitch, are used in traditional floral Chinese appliqué. Other embroidery stitches are used to add detail.

show off skilled needlework. The Baltimore bride quilts were the most spectacular of these.

The Depression years of the 1930s meant a revival of the thrift element in appliqué, and new patterns developed. Earlier designs had been based on natural forms – wild roses, ferns, feathers and honeysuckles – but new, more urban forms began to be incorporated. Contemporary album quilts provide a fascinating record of day-to-day life, with silhouette cut-outs of such mundane objects as teapots, shoes, scissors, bottles and table-lamps. Inspiration also came from the outside world and current events. One quilt made in 1939 has a dramatic appliqué design of aircraft, to commemorate Lindbergh's transoceanic flight.

Appliqué has a fascinating inter-national heritage which is not fixed in the past. New materials such as iron-on fusible bonding and interfacing means that a wide range of fabrics can now be used to create projects that will take this ancient craft into a new century.

Right: A variety of appliqué and embroidery techniques has been cleverly incorporated into this recreation of a child's drawing.

by missionaries, who provided the local people with cloth and thread. They brought with them the customs of American patchwork and appliqué, which use small pieces of fabric. The Hawaiian women, however, had no history of re-using scraps and so cut out large, quilt-sized motifs from single sheets of folded cloth. Their imagery was drawn from their island surroundings: grape vines, seaweed, coral, palms and luxurious tropical flowers in vibrant colours such as fuchsia, jade and deep sea green.

It is in America, however, that the most famous tradition grew up. The early settlers made quilts primarily to

keep warm as they moved westward. On the Eastern seaboard, as life became more stable, there was more time to sew. Complicated appliqué star, foliage and plume patterns evolved and appliqué became a virtuoso way to

Almost any fabric can be used for appliqué: a rough textured white towelling was chosen to make the body of this charming goose design.

125

Appliqué
Tools and Materials

A ppliqué techniques are closely related to, and often combined with, patchwork and quilting, which means that essentially the same materials and tools are required for all three crafts.

FABRICS
In addition to the printed and patterned cottons used for patchwork, there are many unusual fabrics that can be used for applied decoration which would not be suitable for piecing. Metallic organzas (organdies), translucent sari fabrics, "Fortuny"-style pleated synthetics, velvets and textured weaves are all ideal for experimental work. Individual floral or geometric motifs can be cut from furnishing fabrics. Craft fabrics – printed with special designs for patchwork and appliqué – can be used to make personal Christmas or other gifts. Brightly coloured felts lend themselves naturally to this type of work, as they do not fray. Iron-on interfacing is useful to back and strengthen fabrics and iron-on fusible bonding is an effective way of attaching cut-out shapes to a background fabric.

Iron-on interfacing.

THREADS
Sewing thread is used for tacking (basting) and for slip stitching down appliquéd shapes. Hand embroidery in a variety of threads can add interest and disguise raw edges, while machine satin stitch gives a tidy border. Striped or metallic threads are particularly effective.

TOOLS AND EQUIPMENT
Sharp fabric scissors with both long and short blades are necessary for accurate cutting of appliquéd shapes. Fine pins will hold work together before stitching – make sure they do not rust. Dressmaker's pens or chalk or carbon will be needed for transferring templates to fabric.

Dressmaker's carbon.

Dressmaker's fading pen.

Dressmaker's pins.

Dressmaker's shears.

Needles.

Small sharp scissors.

Printed and woven cottons.

Felt.

Metallic and velvet fabrics.

Craft fabrics.

Machine embroidery threads.

Sewing thread.

Striped machine threads.

Embroidery threads.

Traditional Hand Techniques

The basic hand appliqué techniques have been used by generations of quilt-makers to produce a wealth of naturalistic and geometric patterns. These should be worked in closely woven fabrics of similar weight, such as percale or cotton lawn, which are easy to handle. It is important to match the grain of the cut-out motifs with that of the background to reduce stress on the fabric.

BASIC METHOD

Some workers use a quilting hoop to maintain an even tension across the background fabric, but this is a personal preference; if the pieces are pressed and tacked (basted) properly, and the stitching is even, there should be no risk of puckering. There are many pattern source books for those who want to recreate traditional designs. These are usually illustrated at actual size and a turning allowance of approximately 6mm (¼in) has to be added all round. Trace the template on to thin cardboard. Cut out and draw around it onto the fabric. Draw a second line 6mm (¼in) beyond this outline and cut around it. Fold the edge under, back to the inner line, and tack (baste). Clip the curves, if necessary, to reduce bulk. Tack (baste) on to the background fabric, then stitch down. Press and remove the tacking (basting) thread.

CURVED LINES

Thin lines such as those used for stems are cut on the bias so that they lie flat.

1 To make a stem 3mm (⅛in) wide, cut a 10mm (⅜in) strip of fine cotton fabric diagonally across the grain. Finger-press and tack (baste) down a narrow hem along each edge.

2 Bias strips are very flexible and can be interwoven to form intricate patterns as they are tacked (basted) into place.

Left: The strong curved shape of the serpent that encircles this contemporary Egyptian design has been emphasized with an outline of couched black thread, and fine detail has been added with back stitch.

CURVES AND CIRCLES

The curved sides of symmetrical shapes such as hearts and circles must be smooth and regular. One way to be sure of a professional finish is to press the cut-out shape over backing paper before sewing it down.

1 Cut out the shape, including the seam allowance. Cut a second template from paper, then tack (baste) the fabric over it, gathering slightly around the curves and clipping into the point at the inside corner.

2 Press from the wrong side with a hot iron.

3 Take out the tacking (basting) stitches and remove the backing paper. Tack (baste) the shape on to the backing fabric and stitch down. Make a few close stitches at the top of the heart to prevent fraying.

POINTS AND ANGLES

The surplus fabric at the outside corners should be mitred to give a neat finish.

1 Fold down the corner and trim the point.

2 Fold in the two adjacent sides and tack (baste) down, gathering slightly if they are curved.

Above: Appliqué does not always have to obey the rules. The folk-art appeal of this bird relies upon the designer's deliberate disregard for formal technique. The shapes are cut from a sophisticated selection of matching checks, but sewn down with naive bold stitches.

STITCHING

The individual elements of the design should be tacked (basted) into place, then sewn down, using a matching sewing thread and small, almost invisible slip stitches. Working from right to left, knot the thread and bring the needle through the outside edge. Pick up a few threads of the adjacent backing fabric, then slip the needle through the folded edge for 3mm (⅛in). Bring the needle out and pull tight. Finish off securely and remove the tacking (basting).

Above: The raw edges of the fabric have also been used as a feature in this American flag, which makes good use of printed and woven cotton.

Left: The order of assembling the separate elements should be planned carefully before starting, and it is helpful to number the pieces. The outside edges of the four segments that make up the inner circle of this design were sewn down last to conceal the raw ends of the stems.

Printed Fabric Appliqué

The idea of cutting motifs and pictures from printed fabrics and reassembling them to form a new decorative image is a very old one. In the eighteenth century it was known as Broderie Perse, after the elaborate floral chintzes and cretonnes that were imported from the East. Such materials were highly prized for their rarity so, for reasons of economy, individual birds, flowers and/or leaves were cut out from them.

These were then pasted on to a background fabric, in a new arrangement, and stitched in place, to make bedcovers or wallhangings.

This textile version of découpage is even easier to put into practice today; there is an enormous range of printed fabrics available, and new chemical solutions to prevent cut edges from fraying can be found in most craft shops and department stores.

1 Following the manufacturer's instructions, apply anti-fraying solution around the outline of the selected motif and allow to dry thoroughly.

2 Use a pair of sharp embroidery scissors to cut out the shape.

3 Sew on to the background fabric with a small neat stitch in matching thread. This collage technique is not really suitable for garments or items that might receive heavy wear, but is ideal for decorative panels or pictures.

4 It is possible to cut very fine details from treated fabric. This heavy furnishing satin is printed with an intricate paisley pattern.

An assortment of old and new fabrics, all printed with roses, was used to create this floral spray. These fabrics ranged from acetate headscarves of the 1950s and souvenir handkerchiefs, to a Provençale cotton print and contemporary dressmaking materials. Visual cohesion is given to the design by the careful selection of motifs from within a narrow colour range.

Lace Appliqué

A natural progression from using printed fabrics for appliqué is to cut out separate motifs from lace. Anti-fraying solutions are very effective when used on sheer and fine materials, and lace is particularly suitable. Choose machine-made lace with a design that has a clearly defined pattern. Guipure lace, with its strong floral designs, is ideal for this. Old and new lace can be mixed, and the subtle shades blend together well. This form of appliqué is the perfect way to utilize some of the odds and ends of trimmings that gather in every sewing box.

1 Collect scraps of lace, then apply a thin layer of anti-fraying solution to the edge of the most interesting motifs. The lace should not discolour, but it will become slightly stiffer to the touch.

2 Leave to dry, then cut out the individual motifs with sharp embroidery scissors.

Above: Reminiscent of a Victorian paper Valentine card, this pink satin heart is surrounded by lace motifs, appliquéd on to a background of floral cotton lawn. The inner circle is made up of fragments cut from a damaged length of antique lace, which has been washed to restore its original crisp white appearance.

3 Sew the lace on to a backing using matching thread and small tidy stitches. A sheer or openweave fabric gives a light airy feel to the work. This technique could be used to make a romantic border for a bride's veil.

4 Try experimenting with different background fabrics, which can change the appearance of the work; here the net has been appliquéd on to toning satin, and seed pearls added.

In a different mood, these lace motifs have been stitched on to fine habutai silk and a cotton fabric, which has been screen- and transfer-printed with multi-layered images. They add texture and a feeling of nostalgia to the piece.

Using Fusible Bonding

S mall motifs can be easily stitched on to a
background fabric and will lie smoothly
on the surface, but bigger shapes need to have
extra support to keep them flat. Iron-on fusible
bonding is an ideal way to fix two layers of fabric
together. It consists of a soft web of heat-activated
adhesive attached to greaseproof paper. The result
is permanent, hard-wearing and washable – ideal
for decorating garments or soft furnishings.

1 Select a motif from
patterned fabric and cut
out roughly.

2 Cut a piece of fusible
bonding to size and
iron firmly on to the back
of the motif, with the paper
side upwards, until the
adhesive has melted.

3 Allow to cool, then
trim away the surplus
fabric, cutting carefully
around the outline. Peel
away the backing paper.

4 Place the motif on the
background material
and iron according to the
manufacturer's instructions.
Press (do not slide) for about
fifteen seconds with a hot
dry iron.

This exuberant figure is appliquéd in plain cotton fabrics.
The main pieces have been attached to the backing with
fusible bonding and outlined with machine stitching. The
details are hand-embroidered.

Flying cherubs have been cut from Christmas craft fabric
and bonded on to contrasting backgrounds to make these
engaging greetings cards.

5 The raw edge of the motif will not fray now, but it can
be neatened with a decorative line of machine satin
stitch. Adjust the setting to a close zigzag and sew carefully,
ensuring that the stitching is worked half on the motif and
half on the backing fabric. A transparent foot, if supplied
with the machine, makes it easier to guide the fabric. Pull
the ends of thread through to the back and tie off.

Reverse Machine Appliqué

Reverse appliqué is an interesting variation on the basic technique. Instead of building up separate elements on a background material, the design is created by stitching several contrasting fabrics together and then parts of them are cut away to reveal underlying layers. There are long traditions of this branch of textile art around the world, many of which involve intricate hand stitching. Dramatic and effective results can, however, be achieved quickly by using a sewing machine.

Right: Different weights and textures of fabric have been mixed for this sunburst cushion (pillow). The soft pile of the velvet contrasts with the two shades of metallic organza (organdy) for a luxurious result. The width of the zigzag has been varied to emphasize the design, and a feeling of depth is given by stitching with both dark and light threads.

1 Select a design – bold graphic shapes are best – and work out in advance where the various colours will appear. A maximum of four colours should be used in any one design; any more may prove difficult to handle. Trace the outline on to thin paper. Cut similar size pieces of fabric and stack them so that the least-used colours are at the bottom. Place the pattern on top and tack (baste) through all the layers; be sure they all lie flat.

2 Set the sewing machine to a medium-length straight stitch and sew accurately over the pattern outline. Gently tear away the tissue paper without pulling the thread.

3 Using a pair of sharp pointed embroidery scissors, begin to cut away the fabric. Cut just inside the stitch line, leaving a very narrow margin, and be careful not to snip the stitches.

4 Sew over the outline a second time using a broad satin stitch in a contrasting thread. The stitch can be tapered at points or sharp angles by adjusting the width. Be sure that the stitching covers the raw edges on both sides of the line, trimming them back further if necessary. Neaten the finished piece by pulling the ends of thread through to the back and tying them.

Felt Appliqué

Felt is a long-established favourite for appliqué; it is easy to handle and, because it is not woven, it does not fray. Detailed motifs can be cut freehand or from templates, then tacked (basted) down and attached to the background with a machine zigzag or a hand embroidery stitch. Using iron-on fusible bonding saves time and gives a professional effect; the pattern is drawn directly on to the paper backing, so the shapes are always accurate.

1 Trace the separate elements of the design on to the bonding, allowing for any overlap. Remember that the finished pattern will have to be reversed if it is not symmetrical.

2 Roughly cut out each shape and place them, paper side up, on felt of the appropriate colour. Cover with a damp cloth and iron on using a pressing action.

3 When the felt has cooled and the adhesive set, cut out accurately around the outline.

4 Peel off the backing paper. Fix down the background shapes first, again using a pressing cloth and a medium heat setting. Build up the rest of the design, one piece at a time.

Above: Many kinds of decoration or detail can be added to felt appliqué. This confetti-like garland was inspired by the shapes of Japanese cookie cutters. The individual flowers are sewn with contrasting threads, and finished with tiny pearl beads.

Above: In the nineteenth century, felt was used to make ornamental table covers to protect polished wooden furniture from everyday wear. These often combined patchwork and appliqué, and were embellished with embroidery. Flowers and hearts were especially popular and this motif is adapted from a cloth made in the north of England. The raised petals and the leaves are edged with blanket stitch worked in a single strand of crewel yarn.

Reverse Felt Appliqué

The non-fraying qualities of felt make it ideal for reverse appliqué because there is no need to turn under or conceal the raw edges of the fabric. More layers can be used and more colours introduced: the technique example uses four pieces of felt. Small, sharp embroidery scissors are essential for cutting through the felt – the curved blades of nail scissors are suitable for the finest detail.

Right: This three-dimensional nursery rhyme illustration is deceptively naive in appearance; the method used to produce it is innovative and skilful. Seven different colours of felt have been used and, as the layers have been cut into, a great feeling of depth has been produced.

1 Pin and tack (baste) the felt together, with white on the bottom, then blue, pink and a slightly larger square of black. Transfer the design on to the white layer. With black thread sew along the guides and around the outer edge of the square in straight stitch. This stitching needs to be strong, so it worth going over the outline twice. Fasten the ends securely on the white side.

2 Turn the work over so the black side is facing. Cut away the first layer, as close to the stitched lines as possible, so that the felt that is left forms a thin neat line, defining the design.

3 Remove more of the felt from other parts of the design, cutting through either one or two layers to reveal the colours below.

4 Stitch in the fine detail by hand. Cut-out flowers can be added to the background. Sew down in the centre only, using French knots in contrasting thread, to give a raised effect.

Pattern Cut Appliqué

The simple fold and cut techniques that are used by children to make snowflakes and paper chains have been adapted by quilt-makers all over the world. The resulting designs are striking and symmetrical, and relatively quick to sew. The best known of these whole-cloth appliqués are Hawaiian quilts which are cut from a single sheet of fabric. This technique can be simplified to produce bold and interesting patterns. Solid colours on a white background are most effective. Spend time experimenting with different designs, remembering not to cut through the folds and to leave a narrow turning around the edges. Soft curves and flowing lines are easiest to work with and fine-weave cottons the best choice of fabric.

Above: Two vibrantly opposed colours are used for this Egyptian appliqué, which draws its imagery from Islamic art. The design has been cut from several pieces of blue cotton, appliquéd onto a contrasting pink background cloth.

1 This eight-pointed daisy medallion is taken from a turkey red and white coverlet, made in Ireland during the 1870s. Start by folding the top fabric in half, then into quarters, then eighths.

2 Pin a pattern template to the folded fabric and cut out.

3 Turn under a seam allowance of 6mm (¼in) all round and tack (baste) down.

4 Pin, then tack (baste) to the background fabric, ensuring that the motif lies flat. Sew down with small slip stitches in a matching thread.

Left: This Indian cushion cover is made from two pieces of cloth: a dark background fabric and a fine white cotton which has been folded into squares and cut to produce a geometric repeat pattern. Large canopies and bedspreads are made in this way.

San Blas Appliqué

The most complex form of reverse appliqué is South American seminole work, a multicoloured technique developed by the women of the San Blas Islands, off the Panamanian coast. It was originally worked in small panels known as *mola* cloth and used to decorate garments, but is now made for export as a more commercial concern. The imagery used is pictorial, derived from mythology, folklore and the makers' natural surroundings. Up to ten different colours can appear in a single piece; a simplified way of working is illustrated.

1 Tack (baste) the first two layers together and transfer the design to the top. Thin fabrics which do not fray easily, such as cotton lawn, should be used

and they should all be of a similar weight. The darkest colours are placed towards the top, to prevent the turned-under edges from showing through. Tack (baste) around either side of the outline, then cut along it with sharp-pointed embroidery scissors.

2 Using the point of the needle to turn under a narrow hem, slip stitch the edges of the top fabric to the layer below.

Above: The gently curving lines of this stylized fish are suited to reverse appliqué. These are echoed by the shape of the formalized blue waves, which are made from lightly padded bias strips. The slit and circle background patterns are typical of San Blas work.

3 Tack (baste) the third colour to the top of the work and, feeling through the cloth, trace over the hemmed edge of the main shape. Cut out around this outline to expose the two layers below. Turn under the raw edges as before.

4 Ordinary hand appliqué can be used to add detail.

Left: This intricate appliqué was made by the Yao people, a hill tribe of northern Thailand. It uses a cut-away technique, very similar to San Blas work, but the colours are subtler and the pattern more complicated, reflecting differences between the two cultures. Satin stitch is used to emphasize the design and the centre panel is embroidered in cross stitch.

Star-Fruit Panel

The exotic shapes and hues of tropical star fruit and passion fruit are the source of this lively design, which uses the innovative technique of reverse appliqué. Several pieces of bright felt are stitched together and then cut back, one at a time, to reveal the underlying layers. Extra colour and detail are added with machine and hand stitching, using toning embroidery threads. The textured stitches give a sculptured feel to the finished piece, could be framed or made into a cushion (pillow).

MATERIALS

Transfer pencil, or dressmaker's chalk or carbon; pins
Tracing paper
35cm (14in) square of white felt; dressmaker's pins
30cm (12in) squares of purple, yellow, green, pink felt
Cotton sewing thread
Sewing machine; pointed sharp embroidery scissors
Machine embroidery thread in a selection of toning colours and black
Perlé embroidery thread in white, yellow, green and pink

1 Enlarge and trace the design from the template and transfer it on to the centre of the white felt square. Pin, then tack all the felt together, with white on top, then purple, pink, green and yellow. Thread the sewing machine with black thread and sew over the outline in straight stitch. Finish off all the ends securely.

2 Cut into the layers of felt, referring to the main picture as a guide. Keep as close to the black stitched line as possible without cutting into it, and leave an equal amount of white felt along either side of the line.

3 Once all the layers have been cut, extra stitched detail can be worked into the design. Set the sewing machine to the widest zigzag, lower the feed dog, and work random stitches in toning threads over the coloured areas of the panel. This will enhance the effect of the varying layers and heights of the felt.

4 Work the fine detail by hand in perlé thread. Use two shades of each colour to give the appearance of real depth. Work the insides of the passion fruit with French knots and fill in the star fruit with radiating straight stitches.

Cornucopia

The cornucopia is an ancient symbol representing "abundance in everything desired". This felt picture is a reinterpretation of a design from an appliquéd bridal quilt, which was made in the American seaport of Baltimore in the mid-nineteenth century. The bedcovers made there are instantly recognizable by their lavish use of colour and intricate patterns: the women who made them always had access to the latest fabrics and designs from the traders and importers of the town. This modern version uses iron-on bonding and felt, and is quick and easy to make.

MATERIALS
Tracing paper
Fine felt-tip pen; pencil
Paper-backed fusible bonding
Small pieces of felt in yellow, orange, red, light green,
dark green, light blue, dark blue and lilac
Pointed embroidery scissors
35 x 41cm (14 x 16in) piece of white felt

1 Copy the design outline from the template, and enlarge as required, bearing in mind that the finished design will be reversed. Referring to the main photograph, work out which shapes are cut from each colour of felt. Trace all the elements for each colour on to a separate piece of fusible bonding, drawing on to the paper-covered side.

2 Place the relevant tracings on the coloured felts, paper side up. Cover with a damp cloth and press on. Cut out all the shapes.

3 Peel off the backing paper from the iron-on fusible bonding. Following the manufacturer's instructions, begin to iron the shapes on to the backing felt, starting with the the cornucopia. Use the wrong side of the traced main template outline as a guide. Build up the bottom layers first, then the stalks, stems and leaves.

4 Iron on the apple, pear and the main flowers, then add the buds, strawberries, grapes and coloured dots.

139

Goose Shopping Bag

A remnant of hard-wearing checked furnishing fabric is used to make this shopping bag, which is decorated with an endearing goose, complete with its own egg. The goose's body is cut from unbleached plain calico or cotton fabric and the wing feather patterns are indicated using lines of running stitch. A scrap of bright orange chintz is used for the feet and beak. The broad handles of the bag are comfortable to hold when it is laden with shopping. The finished bag measures 50 x 38cm (20 x 15in).

MATERIALS
25 x 30cm (10 x 12in) piece of unbleached plain calico or cotton fabric
50 x 75cm (20 x 30in) piece of checked furnishing fabric, plus 50 x 25cm (20 x 10in) for the handles
Tracing paper
Soft pencil or water-soluble pen
Stranded embroidery thread in dark brown and tan
Scrap of bright orange chintz
Matching cotton sewing thread
Small piece of multicoloured check fabric for the egg
Sewing machine; pins

1 Enlarge the template as necessary. Place the calico over the outline and trace the main body on to the fabric with a soft pencil or water-soluble pen. This is the wrong side of the work. Carefully leaving a 6mm (¼in) allowance around the edge, then cut out the goose.

2 Using three strands of the dark brown embroidery thread, work over the wing and feather outlines with lines of small neat running stitches. Mark the pupil of the eye with satin stitch and a circle of running stitch. Start and finish all the threads on the upper side of the fabric.

3 Turn the goose over so that it is facing to the left. Cut the beak from orange chintz, allowing an extra 6mm (¼in) seam allowance. Turn under the two inside edges and stitch in place on to the head. Clip the curves around the seam allowance and tack (baste) under.

4 Cut out the feet, allowing an extra 6mm (¼in); tack (baste) this under and press. Tack (baste) the left foot in place under the body, then pin the goose on to the front right side of the main bag fabric. Sew the goose down with tan running stitch.

5 Pin on the second foot and sew down with running stitch. Cut an egg shape from multicoloured checked fabric, tack (baste) the edges under and sew in place in the bottom right-hand corner.

6 Cut two strips 12.5 x 51cm (5 x 20in) each to form the handles. Stitch each along the long edge, then turn through and press.

Fold the bag fabric in half, with the appliqué on the inside, then sew along the side and bottom edges. Turn right side out, and fold under 2.5cm (1in) all around the top edge. Press, then turn under another 2.5cm (1in) and sew down with two lines of straight stitch. Neaten the ends of the handles and sew firmly in place.

141

Mosaic Cushion (Pillow)

1 Cut out random geometric shapes from the fabric scraps, selecting the most interesting patterned areas. These should be a mixture of triangles and four- or five-sided shapes. Turn under 6mm (¼in) along each straight side, folding the surplus fabric at the points back on itself. Tack down, then press each shape.

2 Fold the background fabric in half. Place appliqué pieces on one side. Leave a clear 2.5cm (1in) border around the edge and position the shapes so that they fit together in a pleasing pattern. Take some time to move the pieces around to find the best arrangement. Pin in place.

Appliqué shapes with sharp angles or pointed corners are not always straightforward to stitch, so this cushion (pillow) cover is a good way to practise them. Collect together assorted scraps of blue-and-white printed fabric and sew them on to a dark background for a mosaic effect that resembles fragments of china.

3 Stitch the shapes to the background fabric with white sewing thread using small tidy overstitches. Be sure that any surplus fabric has been tucked under at the corners. Fold the fabric in half with right sides together, then sew around two sides, leaving a 12mm (½in) seam allowance. Insert the cushion (pillow) pad, then slip stitch the third side closed with matching thread.

MATERIALS
Scraps of blue-and-white printed fabric
Cotton tacking (basting) thread
33 x 63cm (13 x 25in) piece of plain chintz fabric
 for the background
Dressmaker's pins' white cotton sewing thread
30cm (12in) cushion (pillow) pad
Matching cotton sewing thread

Shoe Bag

All kinds of textiles can be combined to produce interesting appliqué effects. For this project, an ordinary striped linen tea (dish) towel is transformed into a practical shoe bag by the simple process of sewing on bands of ribbon. A wide range of printed ribbons is now available – the ones chosen for this project all have a nautical theme, which is re-emphasized by the brass eyelets and the thick white cotton drawstring.

MATERIALS

Striped linen tea (dish) towel
90cm (36in) lengths of patterned ribbon
Sewing machine; matching cotton sewing thread
10 x 90cm (4 x 36in) piece of lightweight iron-on interfacing
Dressmaker's pins
Waterproof lining (optional); brass eyelets
90cm (36in) length of white cord or extra ribbon

1 Using the stripes as a guide, sew the ribbon on to the tea (dish) towel with a wide zigzag. Start each line of stitching from the same end so that the ribbon does not pucker.

2 On the wrong side, iron the interfacing along one long edge to provide support for the eyelets. Fold the tea towel in half with the appliqué on the inside. Pin and stitch the side and bottom edges together. Fold under 5cm (2in) around the top edge and press. A waterproof lining could be added at this stage to make the bag into a soap bag.

3 Following the manufacturer's instructions, hammer in the eyelets at evenly spaced intervals around the top edge of the bag.
Thread the cord or ribbon through the eyelets and tie the two ends together.

143

Oven Glove (Mitt)

Aconfident handling of unrestrained colour along with the graphic strength of the egg cup motif, makes this essentially practical oven glove (mitt) a decorative kitchen accessory. A pattern of moons and stars makes a pleasing constrast on the other side of the glove (mitt). The main shape is cut from cotton gingham and quilted by hand, then contrasting perlé embroidery threads are used to emphasize the appliqué design.

MATERIALS
Tracing paper; pencil
30 x 41cm (12 x 16in) piece of heat-resistant wadding (batting)
30 x 70cm (12 x 28in) piece of gingham
Water-soluble fabric pen or dressmaker's chalk or carbon; ruler
Perlé embroidery thread in a selection of colours
Scraps of fabric for the appliqué
Fabric adhesive: matching cotton sewing thread
Contrasting fabric for cuff; ribbon for the loop

1 Trace the template and enlarge to fit your hand easily. Sandwich the wadding (batting) between two pieces of checked fabric, pin the pattern in place and cut out two hand shapes. Tack (baste) the layers together.

2 Using a water-soluble fabric pen or with dressmaker's chalk or carbon, rule diagonal lines across each half of the glove (mitt) to make even squares. Sew over this grid with a contrasting embroidery thread.

3 Cut out the appliqué pieces from scraps of fabric and, using fabric adhesive, fix them in place. Use the template as a guide for cutting the egg cup and spoon shapes for the back of the glove (mitt), and make a more random pattern on the palm side.

4 Take the fabric shapes and, with brightly coloured perlé embroidery thread, sew the pieces, using decorative stitches.

5 With right sides facing, sew the two pieces together, leaving a seam allowance of 12mm (½in). Clip the curves and turn through.

6 Cut a 7.5 x 25cm (3 x 10in) strip of contrasting fabric to trim the cuff. Fold in half lengthways and press. Turn under the raw edges, to the centre, and press. Place the fabric around the open edge of the glove and stitch in place. Sew a loop of ribbon to the inside of the glove (mitt) for hanging.

Apron

This bright and cheerful cotton drill apron is bound to enliven the most mundane household task, from tending to the dishes or polishing the car to washing and dusting. Iron-on fusible bonding is used to attach the main motifs, but the smaller shapes are fixed in place with time-saving fabric adhesive. The neck loop and ties are made from one continuous length of tape, which means that it will always adjust to fit the individual wearer.

MATERIALS
75 x 100cm (30 x 40in) piece of fabric for the apron
Dressmaker's pins
Sewing machine; matching machine sewing thread
12.5 x 115cm (5 x 45in) piece of fabric for the tie
Tracing paper; pencil; iron-on fusible bonding
Perlé embroidery thread in a selection of colours
Scraps of fabric for the appliqué shapes
51cm (20in) square of fabric for the pocket
Fabric adhesive
Safety pin
Bias binding; Ric-rac braid (trim)

1 Make the apron shape by cutting away two curved shapes from the top of the main fabric, leaving a 25cm (8in) straight edge in the centre. Stitch a double hem along each of the four straight sides. Fold under a seam allowance of 6mm (¼in) along the two curved edges and press down. Turn under again, then pin and stitch down 2cm (¾in) from the edge, to form a channel for the tie.

2 Cut two strips of fabric, each 6.5 x 115cm (2½ x 45in), and join to make the tie. Fold in half along the length, with wrong sides together, and press. Unfold the fabric, fold the edges lengthways into the centre and press. Fold back together along the original crease, press and pin in place, turning in the two ends. Machine stitch along both sides of the tie to secure.

3 Enlarge the template and trace the large cactus shapes on to the paper side of the fusible bonding. Iron on to the chosen fabric and cut out. Using the main picture as a guide, cut circles and stars from contrasting scraps of cotton fabric. Glue in place with fabric adhesive.

4 Cut two pieces of fabric for the pocket, each measuring approximately 28 x 35 x 48cm (11 x 14 x 19in). Sew together with right sides facing, leaving a small space at one side. Clip the corners and turn through. Stitch the space together with slip stitch and press down.

5 Cut a length of coloured fabric with a wide zigzag edge and attach it to the top of the apron pocket with fabric adhesive. Stitch a piece of coloured bias binding along the same edge. Finish off with a length of Ric-rac braid (trim), sewn down with running stitch.

6 Hand stitch the pocket to the apron with contrasting embroidery thread. Peel the backing from the cactus shapes and, with a damp cloth, iron into place. The spikes are sewn on with green thread using random straight stitches. Attach a safety pin to the tie and thread through the channels, leaving a loop.

Nightdress Case

P added appliqué has a luxurious appearance, especially when worked with lavish satins and taffetas. Printed or patterned motifs are stitched on to a backing fabric, then stuffed with wadding (batting), to give extra depth to the finished piece. This glamorous nightdress case is lined with iron-on quilting, which is quick and convenient to use, and trimmed with silkcord and tassels.

MATERIALS

38 x 83cm (15 x 33in) piece of iron-on quilting
41 x 140cm (16 x 55in) piece of taffeta
Remnant of printed fabric with cherub pattern
Dressmaker's pins
Matching cotton sewing thread; sewing machine
Small piece of polyester wadding (batting)
140cm (55in) length of heavy cord; 2 tassels

1 Using a damp cloth, press the quilting to the taffeta, 41cm (16in) from one short end, with 12mm (½in) at each side. The larger flap of taffeta will later be folded over to form the back of the bag's decorated front flap.

2 Cut out two cherub motifs from the printed fabric.

3 Position the cherubs on the right side of the cover flap and sew in place with satin stitch, using thread to match the main fabric.

4 Turn over, and carefully cut a slit through both the quilting and taffeta, along the length of each motif. Use the point of a pair of scissors to push small amounts of wadding (batting) into the shape, being careful not to overstuff. Sew up the slit, and fold the loose end of taffeta back to cover the quilting. Pin the two sides together, then sew with satin stitch to make a flap.

5 Fold the spare taffeta at the other end back over the quilting, then fold the lower part in half to form the main bag. Pin the sides together, then sew with satin stitch. Trim the raw edges and hand stitch the cord around the sides and flap. Finish off the bottom corners by sewing on the tassels.

Notice (Bulletin) Board

N ew textile processes are always being
developed and can be incorporated
with traditional ways of working to
produce dramatic effects. This *trompe-
l'oeil* notice (bulletin) board is decorated
with a collage of brightly coloured
postcards and uses an inventive technique
to transfer the images on to cloth. The
transfer solution is available from most
craft shops.

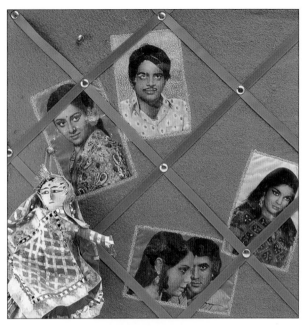

MATERIALS
Image-transfer solution
6 colour photocopies of postcards or photo
White cotton fabric; Cork board plus green
 felt or baize to cover
Iron-on fusible bonding
Sewing machine; machine embroidery
 thread in gold; embroidery hoop
Drawing pins; thumb tacks

1 Following the
instructions,
transfer the
photocopied
images on to the
white fabric. Most
processes suggest
that the image
dries for 24 hours
and is then fixed
with a hot iron.

2 Cut the
green felt or
baize to fit the
board, allowing
5cm (2in) extra
around each edge.
Trim the surplus
fabric from
around the
transferred
images.

3 Cut a piece
of iron-on
fusible bonding
the same size as
each of the
postcard images.
Iron the adhesive
side on to the
reverse of each
image, then peel
off the backing
paper. Arrange the postcards and iron on to the felt, using a
piece of cloth to protect the images.

4 Put the felt
in an
embroidery hoop
and machine
stitch lines of
straight or satin
stitch in gold
around each
image. Fix the felt
to the board
using tacks, at the
back. Fasten lengths of ribbon across the board to form a
lattice, securing the intersections with drawing pins.

149

Tartan (Plaid) Throw

The informality of floral chintz and the geometric patterns of tartan fabrics work well together, and the combination has a traditional country-house feel to it. This versatile throw is made from a length of woven furnishing-weight tartan (plaid) with a lavish swag of flowers and leaves appliquéd across one corner, and a smaller arrangement at the opposite end. The flowered fabric came from an upholsterer's old sample book – a good source of different patterns and colourways.

MATERIALS
Remnants of floral chintz fabric
90cm (36in) iron-on fusible bonding
137 x 152cm (54 x 60in) piece of woven tartan
  (plaid) furnishing fabric
Dressmaker's pins
Sewing machine
Various matching machine sewing threads
Decorative furnishing braid (optional)

1 Sort through the remnants of the chintz fabric and select the most eye-catching leaves and flowers. Cut a rough shape from fusible bonding for each and iron on to the back of the fabric. Cut out, leaving a narrow margin around the edge.

2 Peel off the backing paper. Lay the flowers out on the tartan fabric, taking some time to arrange them into a pleasing pattern. Overlap some of the individual shapes and use separate leaves to fill in any spaces.

3 Once a final arrangement has been decided, iron the shapes down, being careful not to move them out of place. It may help to pin the flowers down before pressing them.

4 Thread the sewing machine with green thread and set to a wide close satin stitch. Sew around all the raw leaf edges, varying the shades of the thread to match the different fabrics. Use pinks and reds to edge the flowers.

5 When the appliqué is complete, trim the tartan (plaid) fabric so that the edges are square and fray along each side to form a narrow fringe. Some fabrics may not unravel easily, in which case a decorative furnishing braid could be used to trim the throw.

Bolster Pillow

Appliqué can be used to subtle effect by combining fabrics in a similar colour range, but with contrasting textures. The bolster cover is constructed from reverse appliqué, in which two pieces of fabric are stitched together and parts of the upper layer cut away to reveal the cloth below. The pillow would fit into any interior design scheme and look at home in an understated modern environment, or piled on a sofa amidst brocade and velvet cushions.

MATERIALS
65 x 90cm (26 x 36in) white cotton fabric
51 x 65cm (20 x 26in) cream cotton fabric
Dressmaker's pins; cotton tacking (basting) thread
Dressmaker's chalk or carbon
Thin cardboard; pencil
White cotton sewing thread; sewing machine
45cm (18in) bolster pad
90cm (36in) length of ribbon

1 Cut a 51 x 65cm (20 x 26in) piece of white fabric and place over the cream fabric, aligning the weave. Pin together, then tack (baste) a grid of 9cm (3½in) squares across the surface. Enlarge and transfer the template design on to thin cardboard and cut out. Draw the triangular pattern on to the fabric, reversing the template either side of the tacked line.

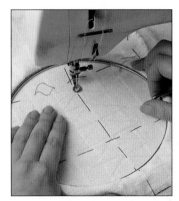

2 With white cotton sewing thread, machine straight stitch over the chalk marks to outline the triangles.

3 Carefully cut away the top layer of fabric within the stitching. Set the machine to zigzag and work satin stitch over the straight stitch to cover the raw edges. Repeat until the entire cloth has been appliquéd.

4 Cut the rest of the white fabric in two long strips, and mark a zigzag border, 10cm (4in) deep, along one long edge of each. Sew with straight stitch and cut out close to the stitching. Work satin stitch over the raw edges.

5 Sew one frilled piece to each end of the main piece and fold in half lengthways, with right sides together. Join along the side seam, leaving a seam allowance of 2cm (¾in). Press the seams open and turn right side out.

6 Insert the pad into the pillow cover and keep in place by tying each end of the case with a length of ribbon, like a Christmas cracker.

Knitting

H and knitting is a skill that can be enjoyed at many levels and most people remember with great affection making their first multi-coloured scarf. Only the most basic techniques are needed to make simple items but, once they have been mastered, there is great scope for creating beautiful knitted garments using the many patterns and yarns that are available.

Knitting

Like all other needlecrafts, knitting has been practised for many centuries, in many parts of the world, although its exact origins are obscure. Textiles have always been made to be used and worn, so little remains from the ancient and more recent past. Fragments of knitted-type fabrics have been discovered in pre-dynastic tombs in Egypt, but it is believed that these were formed by needle-weaving with separate strands of yarn, rather than knitted from a single length. It is known, however, that the nomads of the Middle East spun wool from their sheep and knitted it into intricately patterned garments and tent flaps. These travelling people took their craft from place to place and traders introduced it to Mediterranean seaports, from where it spread to western Europe.

During early times knitting was worked on simple peg-board frames, in the same way that children's French knitting cords are made today. The changeover to using four needles for working in the round came about some two thousand years ago. It was only in later years that metal needles were manufactured; they were first made of sharpened wood, and there

Modern knitting can be very adventurous: these brightly striped hats for adults and children are bold and sculptural in form.

are even records of goose quills being adapted for knitting.

In Europe, by the Middle Ages, knitting had become an almost exclusively male preserve, and women were employed in spinning the yarn. Knitting guilds were established in most capital cities to protect craft skills – and their members were all men. The entry standards were as rigorous as for any other craft; an apprentice had to study for six years to be judged proficient enough to join a guild, and he had to create several items for assessment, including silk stockings, a multicoloured carpet and a felted cap. At this time knitting was closely linked with felt-making. Circular hats were made from thick woollen yarn, which was then washed, pounded and moulded to create a warm and densely textured fabric.

The knitting industry became mechanized well before the Industrial

Revolution, although hand knitting continued in outlying areas where sheep were bred. In the 1600s, the Reverend William Lee invented a machine for manufacturing stockings, which used a ring of latchet hooks. All knitting machines still use the same principle. The first hose he produced were of thick wool, but he refined the machinery so that delicate silk could be made into stockings that met with the approval of Queen Elizabeth I.

As knitting became widespread, distinctive regional and national variations emerged. Cardigans from the Austrian Tyrol were embroidered with spring flowers, while the heavy-duty sweaters needed to keep out the freezing Norwegian winter winds were decorated with reindeer and fir trees. Scandinavian patterns are predominantly white, like the snow, with dark primary coloured motifs, but traditional Spanish knitting, with

The softly muted autumnal shades of this traditional Shetland hat and glove set come from using natural undyed fleece to spin the wool.

coast. Shetland knitting has now developed into a thriving local industry and the fleece is processed and spun on the islands. Most of the knitters work from their own homes to produce garments and heirloom lace shawls, which are exported worldwide. It is only recently that many of the patterns have been written down and charted; previously knitters had learnt them by memory in childhood.

Sailors and fishermen everywhere have always needed to wear practical and waterproof sweaters. The textured motifs usually include anchors, along with twisted cables that represent the ropes and nets which they used every day. The potential of these exclusively male garments was recognized in the 1900s when long, elegant variations of the traditional Jerseys and Guernseys from the Channel Islands were adopted by emancipated women. The ancient cable, bobble and diamond patterns of the Aran islanders, traditionally knitted in unbleached cream wool, have been revived several times since the 1950s, and are as popular now as they have ever been.

Left: The vivid colours of a medieval stained glass window were the inspiration behind this beautifully hand-knitted intarsia design.

Wales, but their origins date back many centuries. Local legend has it that the multicoloured banded designs were inspired by the knitted garments worn by sailors of the Spanish Armada, whose ships had been wrecked on the treacherous Shetland

its North African influence, used the brightest silk yarns with extra gold and silver threads.

The characteristic knitted garments still produced on the Shetland Isles are well known for the expertise that goes into making them. The classic geometric pullovers were highly sought after in the 1930s, when they became the trademark of the then Prince of

The long-established textured Aran patterns of interlaced cables and bobbles have been reinterpreted in soft yarns to make these contemporary sweaters.

Knitting
Tools and Materials

To the beginner, the tremendous array of yarns available may seem quite bewildering. Wools should be chosen with the end purpose in mind but all printed patterns give a recommended yarn, needle-size and tension (gauge).

KNITTING NEEDLES

There are three types of needle: single-pointed, double-pointed and circular. Single-pointed needles are used for most work and range from 2.00 to 10.00mm in diameter; the finest are made from metal and the thicker ones from plastic. Bamboo needles are more flexible and therefore easier on the hands. Large garment pieces and tubular knitting are worked on circular needles. Sets of four double-pointed needles are also used for small circular pieces such as socks or hats. Cable needles carry groups of stitches across the surface of the knitting.

TOOLS AND ACCESSORIES

Stitch counters record the number of rows worked and stitch markers can be slipped over the needles to indicate where a row begins in circular knitting. Use a gauge to check needle sizes – this is particularly useful as old needles were numbered to a different system. A crochet hook is useful for picking up dropped stitches and tapestry needles are used to stitch pieces together and for tidying up ends.

YARN

Knitting yarns come in many colours and textures, and are made from natural, synthetic and blended fibres. Wool and acrylic are warm and practical, and combinations of the two are specially formulated for easy washing. Constantly developing processes mean that new "novelty" yarns are always on the market.

Yarns are classified according to weight – light, medium or heavy – and by the number of threads or plys which are spun together to make the strand. Basic double knitting is a versatile 4-ply wool and 3-ply "fingering" is used for baby garments. Fine Shetland lace is knitted from 2-ply wool which comes in subtle natural colours. Cotton yarns are also made in several weights.

Thick bouclé.

Shetland single-ply.

Chenille.

Cotton yarn.

Space-dyed ya

Double knitting.

Chunky synthetics.

Textured and novelty yarns.

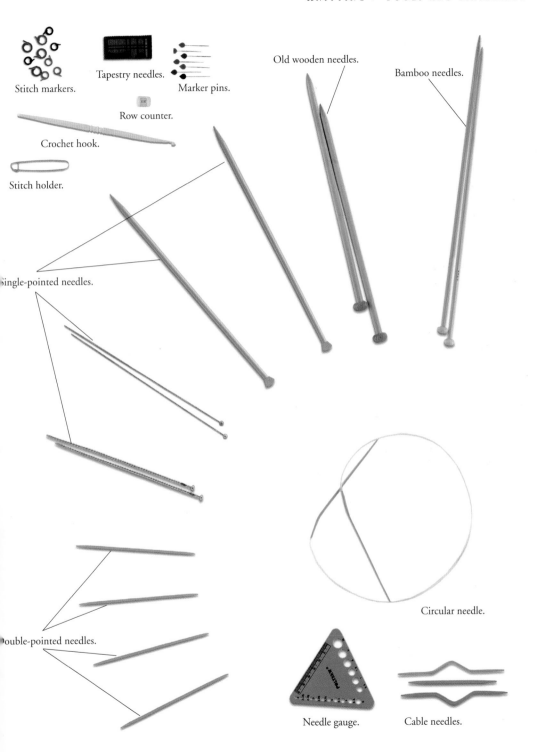

Stitch markers.

Tapestry needles.

Marker pins.

Row counter.

Crochet hook.

Stitch holder.

Old wooden needles.

Bamboo needles.

Single-pointed needles.

Double-pointed needles.

Circular needle.

Needle gauge.

Cable needles.

159

Casting On

Knitting is worked on two needles and the fabric grows as the stitches are passed from one to the other. There are no set rules about how to hold the yarn and needles – knitters in different parts of the world use them in entirely different ways – and, with practice, everybody finds their own personal method. Left-handed workers should use a mirror to reverse the technique pictures.

Plain stocking stitch is all that has been used here to create these exciting swatches, which are knitted from a selection of fashion yarns.

CASTING ON

The knitted stitches are built up on a foundation of loops. The two most common ways of making this initial row are the one-needle and the two-needle method. The first, sometimes called the thumb method, is perhaps the easiest for beginners and gives an elastic, hardwearing edge. Whichever technique is chosen, it is important to work with an even tension, or the stitches will be too tight to work.

Both methods of casting on begin with a slip loop, which forms the first stitch.

1 MAKING A SLIP LOOP Wrap the long end of the yarn around the short end.

2 Use the tip of the needle to lift the main strand through the loop.

3 Pull on the short end to tighten the slip loop.

1 ONE-NEEDLE METHOD
Make a slip loop at the end of the yarn, allowing at least 30cm (6in) plus an extra 2.5cm (1in) for each stitch. Place the loop on the needle and hold in the right hand. Wrap the short end under and over the left fingers and hold securely in place with the thumb.

2 Insert the tip of the needle under the yarn between the first and second fingers, then with the right hand, wrap the long end of the yarn under and over the needle.

3 Bring the needle and yarn forward, under the taut thread, pulling with the left hand to tighten the new stitch that has been made.

4 Repeat the process for the next stitch and continue until the required number of stitches has been made.

1 TWO-NEEDLE METHOD
Make a slip loop 30cm (6in) from the end of the yarn and place on the left needle. Insert the right needle through the loop from front to back. Hold the working yarn in the right hand, keeping the tension by passing it under the middle two fingers and around the little finger.

2 With the right hand, wrap the yarn forward, under and over the right needle.

3 This forms the new loop: draw it through the slip loop with the tip of the right needle.

4 Pass the new loop on to the left-hand needle, next to the slip loop.

5 Insert the right needle through the front of the new stitch, wrap the yarn under and over the tip, then repeat the process to make another stitch. Continue until the required number of stitches has been made.

Knit and Purl

There are just two stitches – knit and purl – which form the basis of all knitting patterns. When a stitch is knitted, the loop lies at the back of the finished work so that the front of the stitch has a flat appearance; when a stitch is purled the loop lies to the front of the work, so that a small raised line is formed.

Above: Garter stitch is the simplest of all stitches and is formed when every stitch of each row is knitted. The work is reversible and has an elastic texture, ideal for blankets, scarves or sweaters.

1 KNIT STITCH The working needle is held in the right hand, in the same way as a pencil. Maintain tension by passing the yarn over the first finger, under the two middle fingers and loosely around the little finger. It should pass through easily. Insert the right needle through the first loop on the left needle, from front to back.

Above: Striped patterns can easily be created by changing the yarn colour between rows.

2 The point of the right needle is now lying behind the left needle. Wrap the yarn forward, under and over the right needle.

3 Bring the point of the right needle forward, down and under the left needle, drawing the yarn through to make a new stitch.

4 Slip the new stitch off the left needle and on to the right. Repeat until all the stitches have been knitted. Continue with the next row by turning the work and swapping the needles over.

1 PURL STITCH
Bring the yarn to the front of the work and across the right needle.

2 Insert the tip of the right needle from right to left through the next stitch on the left needle.

STOCKING (STOCKINETTE) STITCH is most commonly used for garments and has a horizontal stretch. It is formed by knitting one row and purling the next, which produces its distinctively smooth "right" side.

3 Wrap the yarn back over the right needle, from right to left between the two points, and back under the right needle to the front.

4 Slide the point of the right needle down and back behind the tip of the left needle and slip the new stitch on to the right needle. Continue to the end of the row.

REVERSE STOCKING (STOCKINETTE) STITCH is really the "wrong" side of stocking (stockinette) stitch, and has the appearance of a dense garter stitch. It is used as a contrast pattern, particularly in fisherman's sweater patterns.

Following a Pattern

At first glance, any knitting pattern may appear to be just a string of complicated codes, but it is actually set out in a logical and concise form. A standard series of abbreviations and symbols is used to guide the worker through each row of the pattern: those used in this book are given here, although all printed patterns will include their own key.

Read the pattern carefully and be sure of the instructions before embarking on any new project. For the best results use the yarn specified, where possible. Different dye lots may vary in colour so read the label on each ball to make sure they match.

ABBREVIATIONS

beg	beginning
c	cable
cont	continue
dec	decrease
foll	following
inc	increase
K	knit
K2tog	knit 2 together
K2tog tbl	knit 2 together through back of loop
m1	make 1
patt (pat)	pattern
P	purl
P2tog	purl 2 together
psso	pass slip stitch over
RS	right side
rep	repeat
sl st	slip stitch
sts	stitches
tog	together
WS	wrong side
yrn (yo)	yarn round needle (yarn over needle)
yfwd (yf)	yarn forward
( )	repeat the instructions inside the brackets for the number of times indicated
*	repeat the instructions that follow the asterisk

Marker pins and a ruler are used to measure the number of stitches.

TENSION (GAUGE)

It is important to knit with the proper tension or gauge. This does not only mean working evenly, so that all the stitches are regular, but also ensuring that the work meets the measurements given in the pattern. Tension (gauge) determines the size of the stitch, and therefore the finished size of the knitted garment, so it is vital that it is correct.

Tension (gauge) is measured by knitting up a sample using the needle size and yarn specified by the designer and this should always be done before starting to make up any new project. Most patterns name a particular brand of yarn and the design will be sized with this in mind. If another yarn is substituted, it is even more necessary to check tension (gauge) first. The pattern will specify the amount of stitches which, when worked over a set number of rows, should reach a given measurement.

Work up the swatch, which should be at least 10cm (4in) square and pin it out on a flat surface without stretching it in any direction. Measure and mark out the given width and carefully count the number of whole stitches that lie within it. Count the number of rows in the same way. If there are not enough stitches, the tension (gauge) is too tight and needles one size larger should be used; if there are too many, the work is too loose and needles a size smaller should be used. Continue experimenting with different needles until the sample meets the correct tension (gauge). If it does not, the finished garment will be the wrong size and a lot of time and effort will have been wasted.

Knitting Gallery

There are many options open to the imaginative knitter. The selection of patterns available caters for every taste and level of skill. Specialist designers produce kits to make high-fashion garments, but even the plainest knitted sweater can be embellished with embroidery beads. The examples illustrated here should inspire some original ideas.

To create this delicate trellis pattern, pink and yellow crochet flower motifs have been appliquéd on to a hand-knitted background.

The raised texture of these bobble stitch grapes is emphasized by the choice of a velvety chenille yarn in a rich purple.

Traditional Fair Isle knitting draws on the imagery of nature; the geometric shapes on these gloves are reminiscent of snowflakes.

Woven carpets and other textiles from many cultures can be a great source of inspiration for intarsia knitting and the designs can be charted on to squared paper.

Small silver beads and subtle gold yarn provide delicate highlights on this floral pattern, which has a medieval simplicity.

Natural wooden beads have been applied to a textured background knitted from unbleached cotton in a mixture of stitches.

Correcting Mistakes

As with any new skill, all beginners are bound to make mistakes when starting to knit. It takes time to learn how to control the yarn and needles with confidence, and it may help to ask an experienced knitter for guidance. Dropped stitches, however, are easily corrected, or picked up, with the needles. They may slip off if the work is set aside in the middle of a row or if it has been knitted hastily. Sometimes a dropped stitch may go unnoticed and form a ladder, which will have to be picked up with a crochet hook.

1 PICKING UP A PURL STITCH The dropped stitch is corrected by passing the loose yarn back through it.

2 Insert the right needle through the front of the loose stitch, from front to back and under the strand of the yarn.

3 Insert the left needle through the stitch from front to back and lift it over the strand, keeping the stitch on the right needle.

4 Slip the new stitch back on to the left needle, ready to continue with a purl row.

1 PICKING UP A KNIT STITCH The dropped stitch will need to be brought back up to the same level as the rest of the row.

2 Insert the right needle through the front of the loose stitch from front to back, without twisting it, and under the strand of yarn behind it.

3 Use the tip of the left needle to lift the stitch over the yarn, keeping the new loop on the right needle.

4 Place the tip of the left needle through the front of the stitch from left to right and slide it back on to the needle, ready to be re-knitted.

PICKING UP A LADDER
Knit stitch Insert a crochet hook through the front of the first dropped stitch and pull the loose strand from behind through the loop to form a new stitch. Repeat to the top of the ladder and slip the last stitch on to the left needle.

Purl stitch The method is the same as for knit stitch, but the hook is inserted from behind the work.

Casting Off

A piece of knitting is completed by casting off the stitches. This is usually done on the right side of the work and knit stitches should be cast off knitwise and purl stitches purlwise. This is especially important when casting off the ribbing at a cuff or neck edge. If the cast-off stitches are too tight they will distort the work, but using a larger size needle can help to make a looser finish. There are several specialized ways of casting off, but the method shown here is the most common and straightforward.

1 CASTING OFF KNITWISE
Knit the first two stitches as usual.

Above: The cast-off edge gives a neat selvage to the knitted piece. The loose yarn from the beginning and end should be sewn invisibly along the edge of the work.

2 Insert the left needle under the first stitch made, from left to right.

3 Lift the stitch up and over the second stitch and over the point of the right needle. The first stitch has now been cast off.

4 Knit the next stitch from the left needle so that there are two stitches on the right needle. Lift the first stitch over the second and continue casting off to the end of the row. Cut the end of the yarn and draw it through the final stitch to finish off.

CASTING OFF PURLWISE   The method is the same for casting off a purl row: purl two stitches and lift the first stitch over the second as before.

Knitted Pattern Stitches

Knitting has a rich heritage of pattern stitches which incorporates intricate cables, eyelets or raised bobbles, and knitwear designers are constantly developing new ideas. There are, however, many interesting textured patterns that can be created simply by combining knit and purl stitches to produce a textured surface. Moss stitch variations give a firm, reversible fabric while rib stitch gives a stretchy vertical stripe, used to finish the welts (bottom), cuffs and neck edges of sweaters. To ensure a snug fit, it is usually worked with needles a size smaller than those used for the main part of the garment. Horizontal furrows are formed by working alternate stripes of stocking and garter stitch.

Embossed textures show to best advantage when plain yarns, such as natural cottons, are used.

THREE BY THREE RIB This is worked over a multiple of six stitches, plus three.

Row 1 *K3, P3; rep from *, K3
Row 2 P3, *K3, P3p; rep from *
These two rows form the pattern.

RIDGED BANDS These are worked over any number of stitches.

Row 1 Knit
Row 2 Purl
Rows 3 and 4 Knit
Row 5 Purl
Row 6 Knit
Repeat these six rows to form the pattern.

MOSS STITCH This is worked over an uneven number of stitches.

Each row as follows: *K1, P1; rep from *, K1.

DOUBLE MOSS STITCH This is worked over a multiple of four stitches.

Rows 1 and 2 *K2, P2 rep from * to end
Rows 3 and 4 *P2, K2 rep from * to end
These rows form the pattern.

FISHERMAN'S SWEATER PATTERNS

Knit and purl patterns were traditionally used by the women of seafaring villages to ornament the sweaters worn by local fishermen. These garments were the main protection from the elements in the days before weatherproof clothing and had to stand up to hard physical wear. The various ports and fishing villages around the coasts of many countries evolved their own individual variations of diamond, zigzag or chevron panels, which are still design classics today.

BASKET WEAVE This is worked over a multiple of eight stitches, plus five.

Row 1 (RS) knit
Row 2 K5, *P3, K5; rep from *
Row 3 P5, *K3, P5; rep from *
Row 4 as row 2
Row 5 Knit
Row 6 K1, *P3, K5; rep from *, to last 4 sts, P3, K1
Row 7 P1, *K3, P5; rep from *, to last 4 sts, K3, P1
Row 8 as row 6
These eight rows form the pattern.

EMBOSSED LADDER PATTERN This is worked over a multiple of 14 stitches.

Row 1 *K1, P2, K1, P1, K2, P2, K2, P2, K1, rep from *
Row 2 *(P1, K2) twice, P2, (K2, P1) twice, rep from *
Row 3 *K1, P2, K2, P2, K2, P1, K1, P2, K1, rep from *
Row 4 *P1, K2, P3, K2, P3, K2, P1, rep from *
These four rows form the pattern.

WAVE STITCH This is worked over a multiple of eight stitches, plus six.

Row 1 (RS) K6, *P2, K6; rep from *
Row 2 K1, *P4, K4, rep from *, end P4, K1
Row 3 P2, *K2, P2; rep from *
Row 4 P1, *K4, P4; rep from *, end K4, P1
Row 5 K2, *P2, K6; rep from *, end P2, K2
Row 6 P6, *K2, P6; rep from *
Row 7 P1, *K4, P4, rep from *, end K4, P1
Row 8 K2, *P2, K2; rep from *
Row 9 K1, *P4, K4; rep from *, end P4, K1
Row 10 P2, *K2, P6, rep from *, end K2, P2
These ten rows form the pattern.

ZIGZAG This is worked over a multiple of six stitches.

Row 1 (WS) and all other odd rows, Purl
Row 2 *K3, P3, rep from *
Row 4 P1, *K3, P3, rep from *, end K3, P2
Row 6 P2, *K3, P3; rep from *, end K3, P1
Row 8 *P3, K3; rep from *
Row 10 P2, *K3, P3; rep from *, end K3, P1
Row 12 P1, *K3, P3; rep from *, end K3, P2
These 12 rows form the pattern.

Increasing and Decreasing

A piece of knitting is shaped as it is worked, by alternating the number of stitches on the needles. In effect, the width is increased by adding more stitches to the row and decreased by taking some away. There are several ways in which this can be done, depending on the type of fabric being knitted. The effect can be almost invisible, or give a decorative openwork effect.

1 DECREASING *Knit two together (K2tog)* The simplest way of decreasing is to work two stitches together, at either end, or in the middle of a row. The method for purling two stitches together is similar. At the start of the row, insert the needle from right to left through the first two stitches. Knit as usual. This gives a slant to the right.

2 Knit two together at the end of a row by inserting the needle from left to right through the last two stitches. This produces a slant to the left. It creates an invisible shaping and is used for sleeves as a paired decrease, one side sloping to the right and one to the left.

Above: When lacy fabric, such as these delicate single-ply Shetland scarves, is being knitted, the number of stitches must remain constant, so for every one that is decreased, another is created.

1 *Slipped stitch method (Sl1, K1, Psso)* At the beginning of a row, slip the first stitch on to the right needle without knitting it.

2 Knit the next stitch as usual.

3 Insert the left needle through the slipped stitch and lift it up, across the knitted stitch and off the end of the needle.

4 At the end of a row, slip the last but one stitch, knit the final stitch and pass the slip stitch over the knitted stitch.

INCREASING

Increasing between stitches (M1k) The extra stitch for this invisible method comes from working into the horizontal strand of yarn that lies between two stitches.

Bar Method An additional stitch can also be made by knitting twice into the same loop. This does not give as smooth an appearance as the previous method, so it is used at seam edges.

1 With the right needle, lift the horizontal strand between the last knitted stitch and the next and place it on to the left needle.

1 Knit the stitch as usual, but keep it on the left needle.

2 Knit into the back of the strand, to twist and tighten the loop.

2 Insert the right needle into the back of the stitch just knitted and knit it again.

3 Slip the new stitch on to the right needle.

3 Slip the double stitch on to the right needle.

171

Working with Colour

A limitless range of multicoloured patterns, from traditional Fair Isle, to contemporary intarsia or Jacquard designs, can be created by combining different yarns. Stripes are the quickest and easiest way to introduce colour and can be boldly contrasting or subtly shaded. The Fair Isle way of working appears to be very complex, but, in fact, the intricate patterns are cleverly designed so that only two yarns are required in any one row.

JOINING COLOUR AT THE START OF A ROW

This is a quick method of working with two colours of yarn to create a horizontally striped fabric. Any loose ends can be sewn in when the piece is finished.

Above: Multicoloured designs are usually worked from a chart on which one square corresponds to one stitch. These are straightforward to draw up, when designing original patterns, and can be filled in with coloured pencils. Many printed patterns are in black and white, and a series of symbols are used to represent the various colours.

JOINING COLOUR WITHIN A ROW

Intarsia patterns may require yarn to be joined within a row to create new areas of colour. Sew in the short ends later.

1 Insert the right needle as usual at the beginning of the yarn. Leaving an end of roughly 30cm (6in), loop the new colour over the needle with the old. Knit the stitch.

2 Let the first yarn drop to the side, knit the next two stitches with the double new yarn, then knit the rest of the row with the single strand of new yarn.

3 Carry the loose ends of the yarn along the outside edge as the stripes are knitted.

1 Leaving the first yarn at the back of the work, loop the new colour over the needle and knit the next stitch.

2 Working the next two stitches with the double yarn, let the short end drop and continue with the single yarn.

INTARSIA

When two blocks of colour meet within a row, the two yarns must be twisted together to give a smooth finish and to prevent holes appearing.

CARRYING YARN ACROSS THE BACK

When two colours appear in the same row, only one is actually in use at any one time, so the second colour has to be carried across the back. This creates loose strands, or floats, which can pull and distort, so to maintain an even tension (gauge) they must be woven into the work every few stitches.

1 On knit rows, hold the first colour across the back of the work to the left and work the next stitch with the second colour so that the yarn passes over the taut strand.

2 On purl rows, hold the first colour across to the left and pass the second colour over it before purling the next stitch.

1 On a knit row, hold the floating colour out to the left so that the working yarn passes over it before knitting the next stitch.

2 On a purl row, hold the floating yarn up between the points of the two needles so that the working yarn goes across it before purling the next stitch.

3 Be sure that the float then drops clear of the working yarn, while it is being used.

The different yarns in the traditional Fair Isle Symbister pattern are varied from dark to light by "shading in" the colour in interlocking rows of small diamonds.

The back of the sweater shows how the colours are carried across, so that no loop extends for more than three stitches.

Cable Cushion (Pillow)

The hand-knitted jerseys (sweaters) worn by fishing communities evolved a distinctive functional style over many years. They were made from heavy-duty wool, still impregnated with lanolin, to keep them waterproof and to stand up to hard wear. This attractive cushion (pillow) combines the newest indigo-dyed cotton yarns with long-established patterns; the moss stitch and cable pattern are reminiscent of Guernsey jumpers (sweaters) from the Channel Islands. The natural blue indigo dye is also used for denim; so, like jeans, this cushion (pillow) will fade with wear and use. The finished cushion (pillow) measures 30cm (12in) square.

(NOTE: Cotton yarn has very little "give". To ensure an even tension (gauge), knit as far towards the tips of the needles as you can.)

MATERIALS

100g (4oz) indigo cotton yarn in double knitting weight
Pair of 4.00mm knitting needles
Cable needle
33cm (13in) square of dark blue needlecord (pinwale corduroy)
33cm (13in) square of blue brushed cotton fabric
Matching cotton sewing thread
30cm (12in) square cushion (pillow) pad
Cardboard

1 The twisted cable pattern is worked by slipping three stitches on to a cable needle and holding it at the front of the work while knitting the next three stitches from the left-hand needle. The three stitches on the cable needle are then knitted. This is abbreviated as (C6f) for "cable six forward".

2 TO MAKE UP With right sides facing, sew the needlecord and brushed cotton fabric squares together around three sides, leaving a seam allowance of 12mm (½in). Press the seams and turn right side out. Slip stitch the knitted panel on to the cotton lining, using the indigo yarn.

3 Insert the cushion (pillow) pad and slip stitch the fourth side closed.

4 Make each looped tassel by winding a length of yarn round a 7.5cm (3in) wide piece of cardboard about 20 times. Slip off and sew the loop on to the corner as shown, binding the tassel head close to the stitching.

INSTRUCTIONS

Cast on 60 sts.
Row 1 K1, P1 to end.
Row 2 P1, K1 to end.
Row 3 as row 1;
Row 4 as row 2.
Row 5 K1, P1, K1, P1, P7, C6f, P7, (K1, P1) 6 times, P7, C6f, P7, K1,(P1, K1, P1
Row 6 P1, K1 P1, K1, K7, P6, K7 (P1, K1) 6 times, K7, P6, K7, P1, K1, P1, K1.
Row 7 K1, P1, K1, P1, P7, K6, P7,

(K1, P1) 6 times, P7, K6, P7, K1, P1, K1, P1.
Row 8 P1, K1, P1, K1, P5, K2, P6, K2, P5 (K1, P1) 6 times, P5, K2, P6, K2, P5, P1, K1, P1, K1.
Row 9 K1, P1, K1, P1, K5, P2, K6, P2, K5, (K1, P1) 6 times, K5, P2, K6, P2, K5, K1, P1, K1, P1.
Row 10 P1, K1, P1, K1, P5, K2, P6, K2, P5 (P1, K1) 6 times, P5, K2, P6, K2, P5, P1, K1, P1, K1.
Repeat rows 5-10 twelve times. Repeat rows 1-4 (80rows). Cast off.

Basket Edging

Knitted lace is hard wearing, adaptable and can be worked in a variety of sizes and textures. The basket edging shown here is made on a large scale using unbleached craft cotton, but could easily be made on very fine needles with perlé crochet cotton or 2-ply Shetland wool to make a collar or cuff trimming for a garment. This traditional pattern is known as "ten stitch", as it is worked on a foundation of ten stitches.

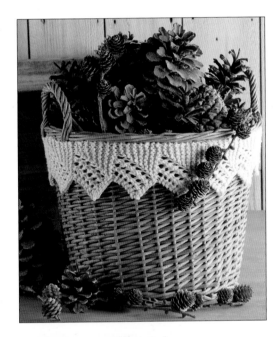

MATERIALS
Cotton yarn in double knitting weight
Pair of 3.50mm knitting needles
Basket
Tapestry needle

1 The open lacy effect of the basket edging is created by repeating a simple stitch pattern: wind the yarn forward once around the needle to make an extra stitch, then knit the next two stitches together. This is abbreviated in the instructions as (yrn, K2 tog).

2 Cast off when the lace is long enough to fit around the basket, ending on row 14 so that the zigzag edge is complete. Join the two edges together neatly and fit the edging around the rim of the basket.

3 Sew in place using a tapestry needle. Pass the needle right through the basket from one side to the other, using small tidy stitches and being careful not to pull the thread too tightly.

INSTRUCTIONS
Cast on 10 st. Rows 1-14 form the pattern.
Row 1 sl 1, K3 (yrn, K2 tog) twice, yrn, K2.
Row 2 and every even-numbered row, K to end.
Row 3 sl 1, K4 (yrn, K2 tog) twice, yrn, K2.
Row 5 sl 1, K5 (yrn, K2 tog) twice, yrn, K2.
Row 7 sl 1, K6 (yrn, K2 tog) twice, yrn, K2.
Row 9 sl 1, K7 (yrn, K2 tog) twice, yrn, K2.
Row 11 sl 1, K8 (yrn, K2 tog) twice, yrn, K2.
Row 13 sl 1, K to end.
Row 14 cast off 6 sts, K to end (10 sts).

Shetland Lace Scarf

S hetland lies between Scotland and Scandinavia, and consists of some 100 islands, set at the crossroads of the North Sea and the North Atlantic. The hardy strain of Shetland sheep has long been bred on the islands, and for over 500 years their fleece has been spun and made into garments. The multicoloured Fair Isle pullovers are famous, but the finest of the single- and two-ply yarns are knitted into lace shawls and scarves. This pattern is inspired by the crashing waves of the seas that surround the islands. The finished scarf measures 90 x 25cm (36 x10in).

MATERIALS
2-ply Shetland wool:
25g (1oz) in white
15g (¹/₂oz) each in blue, pink and lilac
Pair of 3.00mm knitting needles
Tapestry needle

TENSION (GAUGE)
Using 3.00mm needles, 10 pattern rows measure 2.5cm (1in).
Cast on 75 st in white.
Row 1 K2, K2 tog (K3, yfwd, K1, yfwd, K3, K3 tog) to last 11 sts, K3, yfwd, K1, yfwd, K3, K2 tog, K2.
Row 2 K to end.
These two rows form the pattern: repeat five times more and then continue the pattern using the following colour sequence, breaking off the yarn at the end of each stripe.
*
**
2 rows blue
2 rows lilac
2 rows pink
2 rows white
2 rows pink

2 rows lilac
2 rows blue
**
8 rows white
Repeat from ** to ** once
8 rows white
Repeat from ** to ** to complete coloured wave
*

24 rows white
2 rows blue
24 rows white
Repeat coloured wave from * to * once
24 rows white
2 rows blue
24 rows white
Repeat coloured wave from * to * once
12 rows white to finish.

1 It is important not to work too tightly when knitting the three stitches together, so that the right-hand needle can pass easily through all the loops.

2 Cast off loosely and darn in all the loose ends.

3 Pin out both ends of the scarf so that the edges form peaks, then press lightly with a damp cloth. Allow to dry away from direct heat and sunlight.

Baby Wrap

This innovative baby wrap is warm and comfortable for winter outings. It is worked in double knitting yarn and lined with soft cotton. The pattern of geometric bands and child-like figures is knitted from an easy-to-follow chart. The front and back are made separately, then joined together, leaving the convenient zip (zipper) opening along the lower edge. The finished garment measures 51cm (20in) from collar to hem and 28cm (11in) across the chest.

MATERIALS

50g (2oz) double knitting yarn each in lilac, beige,
* purple, turquoise and dark green*
Pair each of 3.25mm and 4.50mm knitting needles
3.25mm circular needle
Stitch holder
2 buttons
2 x 41cm (16in) zips (zippers)
60cm (24in) square of fabric for the lining
Matching cotton sewing thread

BACK

Using 4.50mm needles, cast on 68 sts in lilac.

Row 1 K to end

Row 2 P to end.

Row 3 inc 1, K to end, inc 1.

Work the pattern from the chart, increasing 1 st at each end of the 5th, 7th and 9th rows (76 sts). Carry the contrast yarn across the back of the knitting.

Row 54 dec 1 st at each end of this and following 4th rows until 60 sts remain. Work 12 rows from pattern.

Row 94 K to end of row and inc 20 sts.

Row 95 P to end of row and inc 20 sts. Continue to follow the chart, knitting on these 100 sts for the 17 remaining rows of the pattern. Knit 5 rows lilac. Cast off.

FRONT

Work as for the back until row 105, then decrease for the left shoulder and neck shaping, using the chart as a guide.

Row 106 K45, then put centre 10 sts on to st holder. Dec 1 at neck edge, K to end. Working on these 44 sts —

Row 107 dec 1 at end of row (neck edge).

Row 108 work row without decreasing.

Row 109 dec 1 st at end of row (neck edge).

Row 110 dec 1 st at beg of row.

Rows 111 – 115 work remainder of pattern, and knit 5 rows lilac.

Cast off. Reverse instructions for right shoulder and neck opening.

TO MAKE UP

Sew in the ends and press lightly. Set marks in contrasting yarn 27 sts from the cuff edge on the left-hand side of the front and back, at the centre front and back at the cast-on edge and 5 rows up from the cast-on edge back and front.

2 SEAMS With right sides together, sew along the shoulder seams to the neck edge on the right-hand side and to the marker on the left-hand side.

1 CUFFS Pick up 40 sts on size 3.25mm needles and work 8 rows K1, P1 rib. Cast off rib-wise.

3 NECK Pick up stitches round the neck with the circular needle, starting at the left-hand top: 4 sts along rib; 8 sts along neck edge; 10 sts from holder; 8 sts along neck edge; 20 sts along back neck; 4 sts along rib. Rib these sts for 4 rows and cast off. Sew buttons on to the shoulder fastening.

4 TO SEW IN THE ZIPS Pin the zip (zippers) in the opening at the bottom, then stitch in place to the markers on the lower edge of the front and back.

TO FINISH THE NECK OPENING

Back Pick up 13 sts along from the marker to the neck edge. Rib 3 rows and cast off.

FRONT

Pick up 13 sts from the marker to the neck edge.
Rows 1 and 2 work in K1, P1 rib.
Row 3 K1, cast off 1, rib 4, cast off 1, rib 4.
Row 4 rib 4, cast on 1, rib 4, cast on 1, K1.
Cast off.

5 TO LINE Cut two shapes from the lining fabric 4cm (1½in) larger than the finished knitted wrap. Join at the shoulder, under the arm and along the side seams. With wrong sides together, sew the lining to the inside of the wrap at the cuffs, neck edges and along each open side.

Baby Mittens and Baby Shoes

K nitted bootees or shoes are a popular present for a new baby, and a first pair is often kept as a souvenir. These brightly striped T-bar shoes will fit from newborn up to four months old and are worked in a practical, washable cotton yarn. The matching mittens are made in a basic design with minimal shaping and would be suitable for a baby of up to nine months.

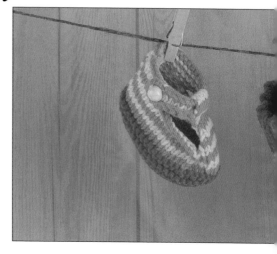

BABY MITTENS MATERIALS
Small quantity of double knitting yarn in pink,
orange and yellow
Pair each of 3.00mm and 3.50mm knitting
needles
Tapestry needle

1 TO MAKE THE CORDS Cut six 45cm (18in) strands of yarn, two each in pink, orange and yellow. Knot together at one end, leaving 2.5cm (1in) of yarn to form a tassel. Secure the knot with a weight, or pin to a fixed object, then plait (braid) to the end. Make a knot 2.5cm (1in) from the end of the finished plait (braid). Brush and trim the tassels.

TENSION (GAUGE)
Using 3.50mm needles, 21 sts and 30 rows measure 10cm (4in) – st st.
Begin at the cuff. Using 3.00mm needles and pink yarn, cast on 34 sts.
Row 1 K2, P2 to end.
Row 2 P2, K2 to end.
Repeat 1st and 2nd rows 8 times more. Change to orange and yellow yarn and 3.50mm needles. Work in the stripe pattern throughout (2 rows orange, 2 rows yellow).
Eyelet row (K2, yfwd, K2 tog) to end.
Starting with a P row, work 19 rows st st.
Dec Row K1 (K2 tog tbl, K12, K2 tog) twice, K1.
Next row P to end.
Dec row K1 (K2 tog tbl, K10, K2 tog) twice, K1.
(30 sts) Cast off.

2 TO MAKE UP With wrong sides together, slip stitch the top seam using the end of the yellow yarn.

3 Turn right side out and stitch along the side seam.

4 Use pink yarn to join cuff. Thread cords through the eyelets.

Row 5 K1, inc 1, K13, inc 1, K1, inc 1, K13, inc 1, K1.
Row 7 K1, inc 1, K15, inc 1, K1, inc 1, K15, inc 1, K1.
Row 9 K1, inc 1, K17, inc 1, K1, inc 1, K17, inc 1, K1.
Row 11 K1, inc 1, K19, inc 1, K1, inc 1, K19, inc 1, K1.
Row 12 K to end.

Change to orange and yellow yarn and work the upper part of the shoe in the stripe pattern throughout (2 rows orange, 2 rows yellow).

Row 13 K17, sl 1, K1, psso, K11, K2 tog, K17.
Row 14 and every even-numbered row, P to end.
Row 15 K17, sl 1, K1, psso, K9, K2 tog, K17.
Row 17 K17, sl 1, K1, psso, K7, K2 tog, K17.
Row 19 K17, sl 1, K1, psso, K5, K2 tog, K17.
Row 20 P to end.
Row 21 K9.

Cast off 9, K5 (including st on needle after casting off) cast off 9, K9. Beginning with a P row, work 4 rows st st on these 9 sts. Cast off.

BABY SHOES MATERIALS

Oddments of double knitting yarn in pink, orange and yellow
Pair of 3.00mm knitting needles
2 matching buttons or beads; tapestry needle

TENSION (GAUGE)

Using 3.00mm needles, 21sts and 30 rows measures 10cm (4in) – (st st).

Begin with the sole. Using pink, cast on 25 sts.

Row 1 K1, inc 1, K9, inc 1, K1, inc 1, K9, inc 1, K1.
Row 2 and every even-numbered row, P to end.
Row 3 K1, inc 1, K11, inc 1, K1, inc 1, K11, inc 1, K1.

TO MAKE THE ANKLE STRAP

Return to the remaining 9 sts, cast on 12 sts (on to the same needle as 9 sts). P across these sts, then P across the group of 9 sts (21 sts).
Work 4 rows st st. Cast off.

TO MAKE THE T-BAR

Return to the centre 5 sts. Beginning with a P row, work 15 rows st st. Cast off.

SECOND SHOE

Make as for the first shoe, reversing the shaping of the strap.

1 TO MAKE UP Join the sole and upper seams along the centre back. With orange yarn make a small loop at the end of the ankle strap and work buttonhole stitch into the loop.

2 Fold the T-bar over the ankle strap and sew the end in place on the underside.

3 Sew the button or bead firmly on to the main part of the shoe.

Tasselled Hat

This child's hat is very straightforward to work, even for the beginner. It is made from the most basic of rectangular shapes and its appeal relies on the dynamic use of colour and the extravagant tassels that add a finishing decorative touch. The size given would fit a toddler, but, once the tension (gauge) has been worked out, it is easy to make the hat larger or smaller. The finished hat measures 35cm (14in) around the ribbed edge.

MATERIALS

Small quantities of double knitting yarn in:
  (A) yellow (B) lime (C) pink (D) bright yellow
  (E) orange (F) turquoise (G) red and (H) purple
Embroidery scissors
Pair each of 3.00mm and 3.50mm knitting needles
Tapestry needle
9cm (3⅓in) piece of cardboard

TENSION GAUGE

Using 3.50mm needles, 21sts and 30 rows measures 10cm (4in).
Using 3.00mm needles and yarn A, cast on 48 sts. Work 10 rows K1, P1 rib.
Change to 3.50mm needles and work the following striped pattern in st st:
6 rows B, 2 rows C
6 rows B, 2 rows D
6 rows B, 2 rows E
6 rows B, 2 rows F
6 rows B, 2 rows G
6 rows B, 2 rows H.
Work a further 2 rows for middle top of hat.
Continue in st st for back of hat:
6 rows F, 2 rows A
6 rows F, 2 rows C
6 rows F, 2 rows G
6 rows F, 2 rows E
6 rows F, 2 rows H
6 rows F, 2 rows B.
Break yarn. Using 3.00mm needles and yarn G, work 10 rows K1, P1 rib. Cast off.

1 TO MAKE THE TASSELS Wind a selection of the yarns used in the hat around the rectangle of cardboard to the required thickness – about eight times for each colour. Knot a length of yarn around the loop and tie tightly.

2 Slip the yarn off the card and, holding the loop firmly at one end, take a needle with yarn through the top of the loop twice and secure. Cut through the other end of the loop, then wind a length of yarn around the tassel 12mm (½in) from the top and tie tightly. Comb to separate the yarn strands. Trim level with sharp scissors.

3 TO MAKE UP Fold the hat in half with right sides facing inwards. Stitch the side seams together and turn to the right side.

4 Attach one tassel securely to each corner.

Fringed Scarf

Most novice knitters start out by making a striped scarf, either for themselves or for their teddy bears. It is still the best way to practise the rudiments of knitting. The yarns for this project are specially chosen in natural tweed-like colours, but knitting a multicoloured scarf can be the ideal way to use up odd balls of wool. A deep fringe gives an attractive finish and can be made to match or contrast with the scarf itself.

The finished scarf measures 25 x 140cm (10 x 55in), but could be made longer or narrower.

MATERIALS
Double knitting yarn in various colours
Pair of 4.00mm knitting needles
20cm (8in) piece of cardboard
Large crochet hook

1 Cast on 50 sts and K each row to end. Work the scarf in random stripes of different widths, joining each new colour at the beginning of a row. The loose ends can be darned in afterwards, or worked in as shown simply by holding them behind the main yarn.

2 Trim the tidied ends close to the work.

3 Cast off loosely when the scarf has reached the desired length. Make the fringe by hooking small hanks of yarn through the finished edges. Wrap the wool about ten times round a rectangle of cardboard and slip off. Insert the crochet hook into the edge of the scarf and draw one end of the loop through the knitting. Pull the other end of the hank through the loop to form a knot. Repeat to the end – about 15 hanks.

4 Cut the looped end to form the fringe and trim carefully so that the edge is even.

Ski Hat

Making a simple garment such as this Nordic-style ski hat in the round, using a circular needle, is much easier than knitting it on two needles. The finished piece has no bulky seams to be joined and all the loose yarn is carried on the inside. The stocking-stitch appearance comes from working in knit stitch only, as the work does not have to be turned at the end of the row. The beginning of each round should be indicated with a stitch marker or a strand of contrasting yarn. The finished hat, which would fit an adult, has a circumference of 63cm (25in). Follow the charts for the Fair Isle stripes in the template section.

MATERIALS

50g (2oz) double knitting yarn each in brown, beige, light grey, cream and dark green
2 x 4.00mm circular needles 60cm (24in) and 40cm (16in) long tapestry needle

1 TO FINISH OFF Darn in the loose ends and pressing the hat lightly. Make the cord tie by twisting together three 60cm (24in) lengths of wool until they fold back on themselves. Knot the ends together to create a loop. Thread this cord through the eyelet holes in the top of the hat.

2 Make a small tassel by wrapping a 60cm (24in) length of yarn around a 5cm (2in) wide piece of card. Slip the hank through the loop at the end of the cord, stitch in place and trim the ends. Repeat for the other end of the cord.

Cast on 96 sts using brown yarn. Work 21 rows K2, P2 rib in stripes as follows, ensuring that the foundation row has not become twisted around the needle.

Rounds 1 and 2 brown.
Rounds 3 and 4 beige.
* Round 5 brown.
Round 6 light grey.
Round 7 brown.*
Rounds 8 and 9 green.
Rounds 10-12 repeat from * to *.
Rounds 13 and 14 beige.
Rounds 15 and 16 brown.
Round 17 light grey.
Rounds 18 and 19 green.
Round 20 beige.
Round 21 brown.
Continue in st st:
Rounds 22-24 brown.
Round 25 (K3 brown; K1 beige) to end of round.
Round 26 K1 beige, *(K1 brown, K3 beige) rep from * to last 3sts, K1 brown, K2 beige.
Round 27 beige.
Rounds 28-32 follow charted pattern 1, reading from right to left.
Round 33 beige
Round 34-39 follow pattern 2, using beige background.
Round 40 beige.
Rounds 41 and 45 follow pattern 1.
Round 46 beige.
Round 47 (K1 brown, K1 beige) to end of round.

Round 48 brown.
Rounds 49-55 follow pattern 3.
Rounds 56 and 57 brown.
Rounds 58 and 59 beige.
Round 60 green.
Round 61 and 62 beige.
Round 63 with light grey, K10, K2 tog tbl, K2 tog, *(K20, K2 tog tbl, K2 tog), rep from * 3 times, K10 (88 sts).
Change to smaller needle.
Round 65 with brown, K9 K2 tog tbl, K2 tog *(K18, K2 tog tbl, K2 tog) rep from * 3 times, K9 (80sts).
Round 66 beige.
Round 67 with beige, K8, K2 tog tbl, K2 tog, *(K14, K2 tog tbl, K2 tog), rep from * 3 times, K8 (72 sts).
Round 68 light grey.
Round 70 brown.
Round 71 with light grey, K6, K2 tog tbl, K2 tog, *(K1, K2 tog tbl, K2 tog) repeat from * 3 times, K6 (56 sts).
Round 72 with brown (K1, cast off 1) to end.
Round 73 with brown (K1, make 1) to end.
Round 74 brown.
Round 75 cast off.

Purse Bag

The favourite Scandinavian colour combination of red and white is used to dramatic effect for this attractive purse bag. Chenille yarn gives it a rich velvety texture which is complemented by mother-of-pearl buttons. The festive motifs of deer and snowflakes make it ideal for Christmas-time, either as a present in itself or as a special package for a tiny gift. The finished bag measures 16.5 x 12.5cm (6½ x 5in).

MATERIALS
50g (2oz) chenille yarn in red
50g (2oz) chenille yarn in white
Pair of 4.50mm knitting needles
Tapestry needle
2 mother-of-pearl buttons

1 Cast on 33 sts and work in stocking stitch. Follow the charted pattern for 54 rows and cast off.

2 Make the button loops on the bottom edge of the finished piece. Using a tapestry needle threaded with red yarn, work blanket stitch into the first 11 stitches, then make a 2cm (¾in) loop, stitch into the next 9 stitches, make another loop, then work to the end. Fold the work in half, right sides facing, and join the two side seams. Turn the bag to the right side and blanket stitch down each side to tidy.

3 Make the cord from two 90cm (36in) lengths of red and one of white yarn. Hold together tightly at one end and twist until the cord folds in half. Make a knot at each end to secure, leaving enough to form a small tassel.

4 Stitch above the knot to fasten the cord to the bag, then sew the two buttons on to the front.

Baby Doll

K nitted toys have a great charm of their own and this engaging baby doll has a very special appeal. He is full of character and certain to delight both adults and children alike. This project is deceptively simple to make: nose, ears, toes, fingers, arms and legs are all knitted separately, using a minimum of shaping, then sewn on to the main body.

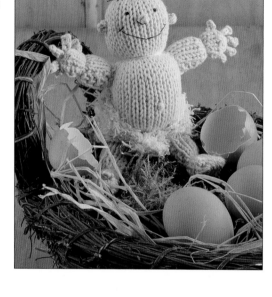

MATERIALS
Pair each of 3.00mm and 3.50mm knitting needles
50g (20g) dishcloth yarn (100% pearl cotton)
Oddment of double knitting yarn for the nappy
 (diaper)
Embroidery cotton in black
Washable polyester toy stuffing
Safety pin
Tapestry needle
Pink crayon

BODY AND HEAD
Begin at lower edge of body. Using dishcloth yarn (crochet cotton) and 3.00mm needles, cast on 16 sts.
Row 1 inc k-wise into every st (32 sts).
Starting with a P row, work 19 rows st st.

Shape for head
Next row K6, (K2 tog) 3 times, K8 (K2 tog) 3 times, K6 (26 sts).
Work 13 rows st st.
Dec row (K2 tog) to end – 13 sts.
Break yarn and thread end back through remaining sts.

ARMS
Begin at hand: cast on 5 sts.
Row 1 inc K-wise into every st (10 sts).

Beginning with a P row, work 13 rows st st.
Cast off.

FIRST LEG
Begin at toes: cast on 10 sts, work 6 rows st st.

Shape heel
K5, turn.
Sl 1, P3, turn.
Sl 1, K2, turn.
Sl 1, P1, turn.
Sl 1, K2, turn.
Sl 1, P3, turn.
Sl 1, K4 turn.
Sl 1, P5 turn.
Continuing in st st, work 14 rows. Cast off.

SECOND LEG
Work as given for first leg, but decrease for heel on last 5 sts on needle instead of first.

EARS
Cast on 3 sts, K1 row. Cast off P-wise. Tie ends of yarn together to form ear shape.

NOSE
Cast on 3 sts. Cast off. Tie ends together to form a small round shape.

BIG TOE
Work 2, as for nose.

LITTLE FINGER
Cast on 2 sts. Cast off.

THUMB AND TWO MEDIUM-SIZED FINGERS
Cast on 3 sts. Cast off.

MIDDLE FINGER
Cast on 4 sts. Cast off.

NAPPY (DIAPER)
Using textures DK yarn and 3.50mm needles, cast on 34 sts. K 1 row.
Dec row K2 tog at beg and end of row.
Next row K to end.
Rep last 2 rows until 2 sts remain.
Next row K2 tog, thread end through remaining st and secure.

1 TO MAKE UP BODY With right sides together, join the seam. Turn to the right side and stuff firmly. Gather up the stitches around the lower edge and close the gap. Tie a length of yarn firmly around the neck and thread the ends back through the work.

3 Sew the arms on to the body, with the body seam at the centre back.

5 Attach the big toe to the end of the foot and sew the legs to the body. Shape the bottom by stitching through the lower part of the body.
TUMMY BUTTON Work a vertical back stitch just below the centre of the tummy.

2 ARMS With right sides together, sew the seam lengthways. Turn to the right side and stuff. Tie a length of yarn around the wrist and thread the ends back through the work. Arrange the fingers and thumb and sew to the hand.

4 FEET AND LEGS With right sides together, sew the seam lengthways. Turn to the right side and stuff. Tie a length of yarn around the ankle and thread the ends back through the work. Using a length of dishcloth yarn (100% pearl cotton), sew back and forth through the work near the end of the foot to form toes.

6 FACE Attach the ears and nose. Work the eyes and mouth in straight stitch, using a single strand of black embroidery cotton. Lightly colour in the cheeks, the end of the nose, the knees and tummy button with a soft pink crayon.
HAIR Sew small loops of black cotton through the head and knot firmly, then clip to form tufts. With a pink crayon lightly colour in the cheeks, the end of the nose, the knees and the tummy button.
NAPPY (DIAPER) Fold on the nappy (diaper) and fasten with a safety pin. If the doll is intended for a child, the nappy (diaper) should be secured in place with a few stitches instead.

Crochet

An amazing range of crocheted items – from chunky hats to delicate lace – can be produced with just a hook and yarn. The versatility of crochet has been exploited by international fashion designers, and crocheted garments are included in many collections. The basic stitches can be adapted to many uses, and unconventional materials, such as raffia or strips of torn cloth, bring a new dimension to a well-known craft.

Crochet

Crochet is an adaptable and enjoyable craft. It can be worked in many different yarns and on various scales to produce a surprising range of items, both simple and elaborate. Its name originates from the French *croche*, or hook, and a crochet hook and a ball of yarn are all that is needed. Crochet is made throughout the world: women of the Mediterranean specialize in fine lace; in parts of Africa it is used to make special caps that denote status, and in China fine crochet table linen is made for export.

The exact origins of crochet are uncertain, but it is known that "the art of the crochet needle" was widespread throughout seventeenth-century Europe. At that time most fine needlework was produced within convents, particularly in Italy. Lace, embroidery and crochet were known as Nuns' Work and highly prized by the outside world. The patterns were based on needlepoint and bobbin lace designs and crocheted in the finest linen thread. The sisters taught their skills to members of the neighbouring communities and crochet spread to Ireland via the church, where it was used to adorn religious vestments and altar cloths.

This Scandinavian-style heart border makes an attractive shelf-edging that would look at home in the bedroom or kitchen.

A flourishing cottage industry existed around the counties of Cork and Carrickmacross, producing Irish Point, Raised Rose and Honiton Crochet. These delicate laces were based on natural motifs: roses, leaves and trefoils. As early as 1743 the Royal Dublin Society awarded prizes for crochet, which was done by both men and women. When the potato famine of 1847 brought economic depression to the country, crochet proved the sole source of income for many people. Some workers were able to earn enough from the craft to pay their passage to a new life in America. Those who remained in Ireland were encouraged to make exquisite lace, which was sold to the landed gentry and taken to London couture houses. Irish crochet was a very popular

fashion item and high prices were paid for extravagant collars and cuffs.

Mercerization processes were developed which gave stronger and more lustrous threads, and more designs appeared. *Beeton's Book of Needlework*, the most celebrated and widely sold manual of its time, was lavish in its praise: "Crochet is easy to work and its strength, durability, and the numerous uses to which it may be applied ensure its lasting hold on the feminine mind."

By the turn of the century crochet was arguably the most popular domestic craft. Lengths of white lace were used to trim petticoats, bloomers and camisoles, as well as outer garments, while crochet lace gloves, bags and parasols were essential accessories. Crochet was not only used

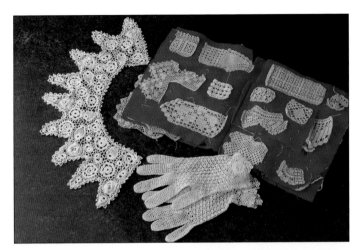

Left: This antique Irish crochet collar and gloves are typical of the fine work that was produced in the nineteenth century. The red flannel sample book was used as a pattern reference source.

the craft was not really revived until the 1960s, when it took on a whole new character. Bright psychedelic colours were used to make mini-skirts, tabards and tank tops. Geometric Op Art motifs were adapted for crochet bedspreads, cushions and rugs.

This style may seem unfashionable now, as the crazes of previous generations always do, but crochet is a flexible medium. Designers are now

Right: Household string is just one of the unexpected yarns that can be crocheted. Simple rows of half-trebles make this functional pencil case.

Above: In this traditional traycloth design, circular flower-shaped motifs are joined together with tiny squares.

for decorating clothing, but was also used in the home to edge blinds, bed linen and dressing-table sets, tablecloths and napkins, chairbacks and doilies. Cotton crochet was hardwearing and withstood repeated laundering and ironing. Many instruction and pattern books were published and crochet was practised by women across all social groups.

Elaborate Victorian designs had been replaced by a more sophisticated style, for both dress and furnishings. Magazine editors dictated plain edges on tablecloths, rather than ornamental scalloped or zigzag borders, while the influence of Art Nouveau was seen in a more naturalistic representation of flowers. Small pictorial motifs were made as insets for traycloths or nightdress cases and narrow ribbon insertions were popular.

Interest in crochet had waned by the 1930s. Functional woollen garments and blankets, cotton dishcloths and pot holders continued to be made, but

looking back for ideas, which can be adapted in a new way, with new yarns, and many exciting and desirable patterns are currently available.

These endearing three-dimensional insects, made from coloured raffia, are an example of the innovative crochet that is being produced by contemporary designers.

Crochet
Tools and Materials

String.

A simple ball of yarn and a hook are all that is needed to begin to crochet. Any wool or cotton yarns can be used, as well as more unusual materials such as string or raffia, but in addition, there is a selection of special crochet cottons for creating more delicate fabrics.

YARNS
Crochet cottons come in balls and are sold by weight. They are numbered from No 3, which is the thickest 2-ply thread, known as craft cotton, up to No 60, which is a firmly twisted 6-ply, used for the finest lace. Space-dyed variations are available for interesting multicoloured effects. No 20 is a thicker 6-ply yarn used for most mats, edgings and traditional white work, but it is also available in other colours. Perlé thread, similar to embroidery thread, has a lustrous mercerized finish. Cotton double knitting yarns form hard wearing fabrics, suitable for bags and placemats or larger projects such as bedspreads. Novelty yarns work up into light and airy garments while metallic yarns come in different weights and colours, perfect for evening wear.

Metallic yarns.

HOOKS
The finer the yarn used, the smaller the hook needed. Like knitting needles, crochet hooks are graded from a delicate 0.75mm up to 10.00mm, which is used for working strip rugs or for creating open, "loopy" textiles. The smallest are made from steel, the larger sizes from resilient plastic. Some workers find that wooden-handled or all-wood hooks are easier to hold. The best hooks have smooth edges that do not snag the wool. In the past, hooks were turned from bone and examples of these can still be found in antique shops. Basic sewing tools are also necessary: a selection of needles is useful for sewing in ends and for joining seams, and small sharp scissors will be needed to cut threads.

Raffia.

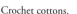

Fine cottons.

Textured yarns.

Crochet cottons.

Cotton yarn.

Fine steel hook.

Double knitting.

Antique bone hooks.

Chunky knitting wool.

Plastic hooks.

Embroidery scissor

Needles.

10.00mm hook.

Wooden-handled hook.

Starting Off

A crochet stitch is formed simply by using a hook to pull one loop of yarn through another. Unlike knitting, where there can be many stitches on the needles, there is only ever one single stitch on the hook, which makes it easy to manage. The thread and work are held in one hand, the hook in the other. As with any new skill, it will take practice to learn how to crochet with an even tension (gauge), but all workers evolve their own way of holding the yarn and hook. Take time to find the most natural movement – and try using a larger or smaller size hook to alter the tension (gauge). The hand positions should be reversed for left-handed workers; it may help to reflect the pictures in a small mirror.

1 HOLDING THE HOOK AND MAKING THE LOOP Make a slip loop by wrapping the main yarn over the short end and using the hook to pull it through. Here the hook is held in the "pencil" position.

2 Tighten by pulling both ends of the yarn. Here the hook is in the "knife" position.

HOLDING THE YARN The work is held between the thumb and first finger of the left hand. To maintain a regular tension (gauge), the yarn is passed back over the two middle fingers, then under and round the little finger. This gives a taut length of thread between the first and second fingers, on which to work, while tension (gauge) is controlled with the tip of the second finger.

CHAIN STITCH (CH)

Chain is the basis for all crochet and the foundation on to which further stitches are worked.

1 Hold the slip loop firmly, then wrap the hook under and over the yarn (yoh or yo).

2 Carefully draw the yarn through the loop on the hook, to form a new loop.

3 Repeat this process until the chain reaches the desired length.

FOLLOWING A PATTERN
All crochet instructions are written with special abbreviations and symbols to make them easy to understand. The most familiar are listed.

alt	alternate	inc	increase
beg	beginning	lp(s)	loop(s)
bet	between	patt (pat)	pattern
chs	chain	rep	repeat
	(chain stitches)	rnd	round
cont	continue	sc	single crochet
dc	double crochet	sk	skip
dec	decrease	sp(s)	space(s)
hdc	half double crochet	t-chs	turning chain
dtr	double treble	tog	together
	(triple)	tr	treble (triple)
htr	half treble (triple)	yoh (yo)	yarn over hook

* Instructions following an asterisk should be repeated as specified.
( ) Brackets either indicate a stitch combination which has to be repeated, or they enclose extra information such as the number of stitches made in a row.

CONVERSION CHART

UK	US
slip stitch (sl st)	slip stitch (sl st)
double crochet (dc)	single crochet (sc)
half treble (h tr)	half treble crochet (h dc)
treble (tr)	double crochet (dc)
double treble (d tr)	treble (tr)
triple treble (tr tr)	double treble (d tr)
work straight	work even
yarn over hook (yoh)	yarn over (yo)

Working in Stripes

Once the basic crochet stitches *(see pages 198–9)* have been learnt, they can be combined to produce many interesting textures, but, with the imaginative use of colour, even simple rows of trebles can be transformed into striped or squared pattern swatches.

Checks and stripes are just some of the effects that can be created by combining colours.

1 HORIZONTAL STRIPES Stripes are created by working in bands of different colours. Join in the new yarn at the end of the previous row by using it to complete the last stitch.

2 The ends of the yarn can be cut off at the end of each stripe and joined back in when needed. The loose ends should then be sewn invisibly into the work.

3 Wider stripes are made by working two or more rows the same colour. When a repeating sequence is being used, carry the yarn loosely up the side of the work.

WORKING WITH TWO COLOURS

Diagonal or vertical stripes are worked by crocheting with two or more colours in each row. The same technique is used for blocks of colour, such as squares, and for more complicated intarsia patterns.

1 The colours are changed within a single row by swapping yarns over on the final stitch of each block. Draw the second colour through with the hook to complete the stitch.

2 Continue working along the row, changing colours every few stitches. The method is the same, whichever stitch is used.

3 Loose (floating) yarn is concealed by crocheting the next row of stitches over it when making narrow stripes; for wider three-coloured stripes, the yarn is carried across the back of the work.

Basic Stitches

There are five main crochet stitches from which all variations have developed. They progress from slip stitch, a travelling stitch which does not make any height, to tall double trebles (triples), depending on the number of loops from which they are formed. When working in rows, extra chain, called turning chain (t-ch) must be worked at the beginning of each row so that the yarn is at the right level to begin the next stitch. It is important to complete each row by working the last stitch into the turning chain of the previous row. This keeps the number of stitches constant and the sides straight. The first row of any stitch is worked through the back loop of the foundation chain, but on subsequent rows the hook passes under both loops of the previous stitch, from front to back, to give a firm fabric.

Clockwise from top: treble; half treble; double and crochet; double treble.

1 SLIP STITCH (SL ST) Skip 1ch, *insert hook under top lp of next ch.

2 Yoh (yo), draw through ch and lp on hook. (1sl st formed).

3 Repeat from * to end of ch. Turn, make 1 t-ch and cont, working the next sl st under both lps of 2nd st from hook. Work the last sl st of the row into the t-ch.

1 DOUBLE CROCHET (DC) Skip 1ch, * insert hook under top lp of next ch.

2 *Yoh, draw through ch only. Yoh and draw through both lps on hook (1dc formed). Repeat from * to end of ch. Turn.

3 Make 1t-ch and cont, working the next dc under both lps of 2nd st from hook. Work the last dc of the row into the t-ch.

1 HALF TREBLE (HTR) Skip 2ch1 *yoh, insert hook under top lp of next ch.

2 Yoh, and draw through ch only (3lps on hook).

3 Yoh, draw through all 3lps on hook (1htr formed). Repeat from * to end of chain. Turn. Make 2t-ch and cont, working the next htr under both lps of the 2nd st from hook. Work the last htr of the row into the 2nd of 2t-ch of the previous row.

1 TREBLE (TR) Skip 3ch, *yoh, insert hook under top lp of next ch, yoh and draw yarn through ch only (3lps on hook).

2 Yoh, draw through next 2lps on hook (2lps on hook).

3 Yoh, draw through 2 remaining lps on hook (1tr formed). Repeat from * to end of ch. Turn. Make 3t-ch and cont, working the next tr under both lps of the 2nd st from hook. Work the last tr of the row into the 3rd of 3t-ch of the previous row.

1 DOUBLE TREBLE (DTR) Skip 3ch, *yoh twice, insert hook under top lp of next ch, yoh and draw through ch (4lps on hook).

2 Yoh, draw through next 2lps on hook, (3lps on hook), yoh, draw through next 2lps on hook (2lps on hook).

3 Yoh, draw through last 2lps (1dtr formed). Repeat from * to end. Turn. Make 4 t-ch and cont, working the next dtr under both lps of 2nd st from hook. Work the last dtr of the row into the 4th of 4t-ch of the previous row.

FINISHING OFF

All work should be finished off properly to prevent it unravelling. After the last stitch, pull the final loop out with the hook, and cut the yarn, leaving an end of about 13cm (5in). This loose end can then be sewn invisibly into the work using a tapestry needle.

Working in the Round

When crocheting in the round, the foundation chain is joined to make a loop. The stitches are then worked into this ring, in ever-increasing circles, without turning. This technique is used to make small medallions and motifs which can be joined together patchwork-style, as well as traditional lace doilies and larger accessories such as shawls or tablecloths. Hats and other three-dimensional items can be created by increasing and decreasing the number of stitches in each round.

Left: Small floral shapes are easy to crochet in the round. These flowers are joined together by the edges of their petals.

1 MAKING THE FOUNDATION RING
Make a short length of chain stitch and insert the hook under the top loop of the last stitch.

2 Join by pulling the yarn through the loop to form a slip stitch.

3 Work the first round into the ring, so that the hook actually passes through it to pick up the yarn.

TREBLE (TRIPLE) CIRCLES

Circles of crochet can be made by increasing the number of stitches in alternate rounds. New colours can be joined on each round and the ends concealed by working over them. Each round starts with one, two or three standing chain, which take the place of the first stitch, in the same way as turning chain.

1 **Round 1** Make 5ch and join with sl st into 1st ch. 3ch, then work 16tr into ring. Join with a sl st to 3rd ch st. **Round 2** 3ch, 1tr into same sp as tr, (2tr into 1tr) to end of round. Join with a sl st to 3rd ch st.

2 **Round 3** 3ch, (2tr into 1tr, 1tr into 1tr) to end of round. Join with a sl st to 3rd ch st. **Round 4** Work (2tr into 1tr, 2tr into 2tr). **Round 5** (2tr into 1tr, 3tr into 3tr).

Right: This sunflower is an introduction to working with clusters of stitches, a way of shaping within a circle. Here they are formed from triple trebles (triples), abbreviated as tr tr.

INSTRUCTIONS FOR TWO OR THREE COLOURS

With first colour make 8ch and join with a sl st.
Round 1 3ch, 15tr into ring, join with sl st to 3rd ch. Join next colour, if using.
Round 2 2dc into sp between next 2tr. 2dc into sp. 2dc into each sp to end, sl to 1st dc (32dcs). Join next colour.

MAKING THE CLUSTER

Round 3 6ch, * yoh (yo) 3 times, insert hook into next dc. Yoh (yo) and draw through (5lps on hook), (yoh (yo) and draw through 2lps) three times (2lps on hook). Repeat from * twice, yoh (yo) and through all the loops to form cluster.

** 9ch (4tr tr into next 4dc to make cluster). Repeat from ** to end of round, sl st to top of 1st cluster.
Round 5 1ch (9dc over 9ch) to end of round. Join with a sl st to 1ch, finish off.

Right: These Irish crochet roses are worked in the round, using a thick Aran wool. They have been appliquéd on to a richly cabled knitted background.

Left: These hexagons are worked from remnants of bright yarn. The stained-glass window effect comes from edging each motif with black, which contrasts dramatically with the other colours.

Crochet Squares

The familiar afghan, or grannie squares, are long-established favourites. The first afghan rugs were made as a means of economizing; at one time yarn was precious and outgrown garments would be unravelled so that the yarn could be re-used. Crochet squares were a practical way of keeping warm, and as a planned colour scheme was then a luxury, colours were used at random. Today, afghan square rugs are still a good way of using up odd balls of yarn, for beginners and experienced workers alike.

Above: This sampler combines afghan square techniques with Irish crochet roses and clusters. It is worked in cotton yarn for a crisp texture.

THE BASIC SQUARE

The squares can be made to any size; small multicoloured arrangements have a jewel-like effect, particularly if edged with a single colour, or one single huge square can make a useful blanket.

1 Make 6ch and join with sl st to form foundation ring.
Round 1 3ch (to stand as 1st tr), then 2tr into the ring, (* 2ch, 3tr) 3 times, 2ch, join with sl st to 3rd ch. Finish off 1st colour.

2 Join 2nd colour to one corner by holding the end of the yarn and pulling a loop under the chain. Work the first stitches over the loose ends of both colours.

3 **Round 2** 3ch, (2tr, 2ch, 3tr) into same space, (3tr, 2ch, 3tr into next sp) 3 times, join with sl st to top of 3ch. Continue the following rounds in the same way, working a 3-tr cluster into every space along the four sides, with two in each corner.

JOINING MOTIFS

Individual squares can be joined together in two ways, by sewing or with double crochet. Hand stitching gives a flat seam, which is invisible if worked in matching yarn, while crocheting produces a ridged effect. All the ends should be darned in securely.

1 Thread a tapestry needle with a 45cm (18in) length of yarn. Fasten on with a back stitch, concealing the end. Hold the squares, with wrong sides facing, and stitch firmly through both loops on each side.

2 Double crochet makes a strong, attractive join, worked through both loops on each side. Squares can be joined singly, or when all the motifs for one project have been completed. Lay them out in the final order, then work all the horizontal, then all the vertical joins.

Left: The centre of this afghan variation is made from eight raised clusters. The combination of chenille and woollen yarns gives an interesting effect.

Left: Hexagonal afghan motifs can be made by working 12 stitches into the first round, two to a side, and increasing in the usual way.

Left: Many variations on the basic square can be worked by mixing the colours within each round. A patchwork block effect can be created by choosing a predominant background colour such as cream, and keeping to a tight colour scheme.

SHELLS AND CLUSTERS

Shells are fan-shaped groups of stitches made by working several trebles into one space. Clusters appear as inverted fans, and are created by retaining the final loops of several adjacent trebles on the hook while they are worked, then drawing them together with one movement. By combining the two, many interesting patterns can be created.

WORKING A SHELL
Insert the hook into the 3rd ch from hook, then work 7tr into this sp. Anchor final st with a sl st into 3rd ch from hook.

Above: These coloured swatches illustrate just a few of the textured crochet fabrics that can be developed by working alternate rows of shells and clusters.

Filet Crochet

Filet crochet is an old technique, which reached elaborate heights in the late nineteenth century. It is still very popular today, particularly in Holland, France and Germany, where it is used to make curtains, tablecloths and figurative panels, as well as decorative edgings. It consists of a regular square mesh, made from trebles (triples) and chain stitches, and the design is created by filling in some of the spaces with blocks of stitches.

This flower basket design was adapted from a pattern that first appeared in the 1900s, when many women led a more leisurely life and had time to work exquisite crochet to show off their skills. It uses a fine thread worked with a steel hook.

1 MAKING THE MESH Each charted square represents 3ch, so calculate the length of the foundation chain by multiplying the number of squares needed by 3 and adding 5t-ch. Work 1tr into the 8th ch from hook.

2 (Make 2ch, skip 2ch, 1tr into next ch) to end of row, ending with 1tr, 5t-ch.

3 For the next and following rows, * 1tr into 2nd tr from hook, skip 2ch, 1tr into next tr, to end, 5t-ch. Work the trs through both lps of the previous tr.

1 MAKING THE BLOCKS A block is made by working 2tr *under* the 2ch of the previous row. For a block at the beginning of a row, make 3t-ch then make 2tr into 2ch 5p, and 1tr into next tr.

2 A chequerboard (checkerboard) effect can be built up by working alternate blocks and spaces. Work the last tr into the t-ch of previous row.

3 When working a block on top of another block, make the 4tr through both loops of the previous stitches.

FOLLOWING A PATTERN

There are many publications which include filet crochet patterns. They are printed on a square grid and are easy to follow. Each plain square represents a mesh and each filled-in square is a block. The first and following odd rows are worked from right to left, starting at the bottom right square, and the even rows read from left to right. For complicated designs, it is worth making an enlarged photocopy of the chart and marking off the lines as they are completed to keep track of how the work is progressing. Many cross stitch patterns can be adapted to filet crochet, and it is easy to draw up designs on to squared paper.

Filet crochet can be worked on a large or small scale, and in a variety of threads. Extra decoration has been added to this simple indigo cotton mesh by interweaving the trebles (triples) with striped braid. This technique would work well on lacy garments, which could be decorated with silk ribbons.

Although not strictly filet crochet, this chenille scarf is worked in a V-shaped mesh variation, which gives it an interesting texture.

Flower Box

C rochet is a very versatile textile medium. Its use need not be limited to wool and cotton yarns, nor only to two-dimensional objects. In fact, with a little imagination and the creative use of brightly coloured raffia, for example, an empty circular Camembert cheese box can be transformed into the cheerful flower-shaped container shown here.

MATERIALS

1 hank each 2 colours raffia for lid and sides
Small quantities of raffia in various colours for the petals
3.50mm crochet hook
Round cardboard box with lid, approximately
  11.5cm (4½in) in diameter
Pencil; silver foil; tape measure; pva adhesive
Sharp large-eyed needle
Sticky tape

1 The box base and lid are both covered with silver foil, which has been crumpled and straightened out again for a textured effect. Draw around the lid on to the foil, add 5cm (2in) all round and cut out the circle. Snip from the outside edge to the inner circle every 10mm (⅜in), then glue to the top of the box lid, folding and sticking the tabs around both sides of the rim. Draw around the base twice, add a 4cm (1½in) allowance and cut out the two circles. Cut tabs as before, then stick one circle to the inside of the box and one to the outside, to cover entirely.

3 Stretch the crochet raffia over the box lid. Using the raffia length, overstitch the cover to the rim. Attach the crochet base to the main box with running stitch. The crochet should reach only halfway up the sides so that the lid will fit.

2 With one of the main colours of raffia, work the box lid:
Round 1 3ch, sl st into 1st ch to form ring. 1 ch, 6 dc into ring, sl st into 1st dc at beg of round.
Round 2 1 ch, 2 dc into each of next 6 sts, sl st into 1st dc at beg of round.
Round 3 1 ch, * (1 dc into 1st st, 2 dc into next st) rep from * to end, sl st into 1st dc at beg of round.
Round 4 1 ch, 1 dc, into each st to end of round, sl st into 1st dc at beg of round. Repeat rounds 3 and 4 three more times.
Round 11 1 ch, 1 dc into each of next 60 sts, sl st into 1st dc at beg of round.
Change to green raffia and work the sides as follows:
Round 12 working into the back loop of each st, work 1 ch, * (1 dc into each of next 14 sts, miss 1 st), rep from * 3 times. Sl st into 1st dc at beg of round.
Round 13 1 ch, 1 dc into each of next 56 sts, sl st in 1st dc at beg of round.
Repeat round 13 once more, or until the sides are the same depth as the box. Finish off, leaving a 90cm (36in) end for sewing.
Make the crochet base using the other main raffia colour and repeat rounds 1-10. Miss round 11 and continue with rounds 12 and 13. Finish off, leaving a long end of raffia.

4 Crochet the petals around the box lid, using a different colour for each petal as follows:
With the inside of box facing, join raffia on to last pink round and work 1 sl st into each of next 5 sts, 1 ch, turn box so that right side is facing. Working back over previous row, 1 dc and 1 htr into 1st st. 2 tr into 2nd st, 2 dtrs into 3rd and 4th sts, 2 trs into 5th st, 1 htr and 1 dc into last st. * ch, turn box around, 1 sl st into each of next 12 sts on previous row, finish off thread.
Working anti-clockwise, with inside of box facing, start the next petal in the stitch on the left of first. Repeat until ten petals have been made. Sew all the ends through to the inside of the box.

5 Make a centre pull for the box lid: 4 ch, sl st into 1st ch to form ring, 1 ch, 10 dc into ring, sl st into 1st dc at beg of round. Finish off, leaving a long end to stitch on to the centre of the lid. Sew the loose ends through to the inside of the lid. Work 8 straight stitches, each in a different colour, around the pull. Trim and tape down the ends inside the box lid and cover with a circle of foil-covered cardboard.

Fabric Bag

This country-style bag uses a technique adapted from rag-rug making, and is crocheted from torn strips of recycled fabric. It is a practical way to use up dressmaking remnants, or to give a second life to the material from an old garment. Cotton or cotton-mix materials provide the best textures. The fabric strips do not have much "give", unless they are cut on the bias, so it is essential to keep the tension loose when working.

MATERIALS

3m (3¹/₄yd) assorted patterned cotton fabric
10.00mm crochet hook
Matching cotton sewing thread; needle

1 Tear the cloth into 12mm (½in) strips, join them together with a few machine or hand stitches and roll each colour into a ball. Make stripes by changing fabric colours as you would if using yarn.

Round 1 Make 4 ch. 1 standing ch, 1 dc in each of 3 ch, 4 dc into 4th ch. On other side of 4 ch make 2 dc, 3 dc in 4th ch. Sl st to 1st ch (12 st).

Round 2 1 ch, 1 dc in same place. 2 dc into each of next 11 dc, sl st to 1st ch (24 sts).

Round 3 1 ch, 8 dc, 2 dc into next dc, 1 dc, 2 dc into next dc, 8 dc, 2 dc, into next dc, 1 dc, 2 dc, into next dc, 1 dc, sl st to 1st ch (28 sts).

2 **Round 4** 1 ch, 8 dc, 2 dc into next dc, 1 dc, 2 dc into next dc, 11 dc, 2dc into next dc, 1 dc, 2dc into next dc, 1 dc, sl st to 1st ch (32 sts).
Round 5 1 ch, 9 dc, 2 dc into next dc, 1 dc, 2 dc into next dc, 13 dc, 2 dc into next dc, 1 dc, 2dc into next dc, 2 dc, sl st to 1st ch (36 sts).
Round 6 1 ch, 1 dc into each dc to end, sl st to 1st ch (36 sts).
Round 7 1 ch, 9 dc, 2 dc into next dc, 1 dc, 2 dc, 15 dc, 2 dc into next dc, 1 dc, 2 dc into next dc, 4 dc, sl st to 1st ch (40 sts).
Round 8 1 ch, 1 dc into each dc to end, sl st to 1st ch (40 sts).
Round 9 1 ch, 9 dc, 2 dc into next dc, 1 dc, 2 dc into next dc, 17 dc, 2 dc into next dc, 1 dc 2 dc into next dc, 7 dc, sl st to 1st ch (44 sts).
Round 10 1 ch, 1 dc into each dc to end, sl st to 1st ch (44 sts).
Round 11 1 ch, 9 dc into next dc, 1 dc, 2 dc into next dc, 19 dc, 2 dc into next dc, 1 dc, 2 dc into next dc, 9 dc, sl st to 1st ch (48 sts).
Round 12 1 ch, 1 dc into each dc to end, sl st to 1st ch (48 sts).
Round 13 as round 12.
Round 14 1 ch, 9 dc, 2 dc into next dc, 1

dc, 2 dc into next dc, 21 dc, 2 dc into next dc, 1 dc, 2 dc into next dc, 11 dc, sl st to 1st ch (52 sts).
Round 15 1 ch, 1 dc into each dc to end, sl st to 1st ch (52 sts).
Round 16 as round 15.
Round 17 1 ch, 1 dc into next 9 dc, 2 dc into next dc, 1 dc, 2 dc into next dc, 23 dc, 2 dc into next dc, 1 dc, 2 dc into next dc, 13 dc, sl st to 1st ch (56 sts).
Round 18 1 ch, 1 dc into each dc to end, sl st to 1st ch (56 sts).
Round 19 as round 18.
Round 20 1 ch, 9 dc, 2 dc into next dc, 1 dc, 2 dc into next dc, 25 dc, 2 dc into next dc, 1 dc, 2 dc into next dc, 15 dc, sl st to 1st ch (60 sts).
Round 21 1 ch, 1 dc into each dc to end, sl st to 1st ch (60 sts).
Round 22 as round 21.
Round 23 1 ch, 9 dc, 2 dc into next dc, 1 dc, 2 dc into next dc, 27 dc, 2 dc into next dc, 1 dc, 2 dc into next dc, 17 dc, sl st to 1st ch (64 sts).
Round 24 1 ch, 1 dc into each dc, sl st to 1st ch (64 sts).
Round 25 as round 24.
Finish off.

3 To make the handles, join the fabric to the top edge of the bag, one-third of the way along from the right-hand side. Make 37 chains and join on to the top edge one-third away from the left-hand side. Turn, and work 1 dc into each chain. Cut off the short end and, with a needle and thread, stitch the fabric securely to the inside of the bag. Repeat on the other side for the second handle.

Baby Blanket and Woollen Balls

This blanket would brighten any nursery and the rainbow colours make it a perfect present for a baby girl or boy. The dramatic chevron pattern is a variation of basic treble stitch, and is quick and easy to work. The matching balls are a good way to use up leftover wool, and can be made in any combination of stripes. They are stuffed with washable polyester fibre, but could be filled with dried beans to make juggling balls for an older child – or adult – to play with. The finished blanket measures about 90cm (36in) square.

BABY BLANKET MATERIALS
50g (2oz) baby double knitting yarn each in red, salmon pink, yellow, green, light blue, dark blue and purple
3.50mm crochet hook
Tapestry needle

1 With red yarn, make a foundation row of 153 ch.
Row 1 Make 1 tr into 4th ch from hook. Make 7 tr into next 7 ch. Into next 3 sts *(yoh [yo], insert hook into ch, draw yarn through, yoh [yo], draw through 2 loops leaving last loop on hook). Repeat from * twice more (4 loops on hook) yoh [yo] and draw through all 4 loops. 13-treble cluster (3 tr cluster) made. 9 tr, 3 tr into next ch, 9 tr*.

2 Repeat from * to * 7 times to end of row. On final repeat work last 2 tr into same ch, turn.
Row 2 3 ch, 1 tr into 1st of 3 ch made, i.e. 2 sts in same place. Work 7 tr. *(1 tr cluster, 9 tr, 3 tr into next tr, 9 tr). Repeat from * to end of row, working last 2 tr into same tr, turn. Repeat row 2 to form the pattern.
Break off the red wool and join the salmon pink wool to the beginning of row for the second stripe.

3 Work two rows of each colour in the spectrum sequence: yellow, green, light blue, dark blue, purple, and repeat the seven-stripe pattern four times, finishing off with an extra two rows of red.

4 Darn in the loose ends of wool. Press the blanket lightly into shape using a damp cloth and cool iron.

WOOLLEN BALL
MATERIALS
*Remnants of double
knitting yarn
3.50mm crochet hook
Washable polyester toy
filling (batting)
Tapestry needle*

1 Make a foundation row of 16 ch.
Row 1 1 ch, skip 1 ch, 4 dc, 8 tr, 4 dc, turn.
Row 2 1 ch, 4 dc into next 4 dc, 8 tr into 8 tr, 4 dc into 4 dc turn.

2 These two rows form the basic pattern and are repeated nine times to form the ball shape. A plain ball can be worked just in one colour, but changing yarn at the beginning of each or every alternate row will create interesting patterns. The top of the tomato variation is worked in double crochet.

3 Use a tapestry needle to gather the two edges together, making sure that all the loose ends of yarn are pushed to the inside of the ball.

4 Sew the edges together with a neat overstitch, to halfway down the seam. Stuff firmly with polyester filling (batting), then complete the seam and finish off the end of the yarn. Roll the ball into shape between your hands.

Strawberry and Tomato Hats

These charming fruit-inspired baby hats could not fail to delight both youngsters and their parents. Stem, calyx and the main part are worked all in one piece, in the round, and the strawberry seeds are embroidered in thick cotton thread. The same pattern is followed for the tomato variation, which is made in a warmer shade of red. The finished hat measures 35cm (14in) around the outer edge and will fit a child of up to one year old.

MATERIALS
Cotton double knitting yarn:
50g (2oz) in red
20g (³/4oz) in green
10g (¹/4oz) in black
10g (¹/4oz) in yellow
3.50mm and 4.50mm crochet hooks
Large-eyed needle

1 Using green yarn and a 4.50mm hook, make 5 ch.1 sl st in 2nd ch from hook. * sl st in each of 3 remaining ch to form the stem.

Round 1 3 ch, sl st into 1st ch to form a ring. 1 ch, 5 dc into ring, sl st into 1st dc at beg of round.

Round 2 1 ch, 2 dc into each of next 5 sts. Sl st into 1st dc.

Round 3 1 ch, (1 dc in 1st st, 2 dc in next st) 4 times, sl st into 1st dc.

Round 4 1 ch, (1 dc in each of next 2 sts, 2 dc in next st) 4 times, sl st into 1st dc.

Round 5 1 ch, (1 dc in each of next 3 sts, 2 dc in next st) 4 times, sl st into 1st dc.

Round 6 1 ch, (1 dc into each of next 4 sts, 2 dc into next st) 4 times, sl st into 1st dc (30 sts).

2 Work the leaves as follows:
Round 7 *(12 ch, 1 sl st into 2nd ch from hook, 1 sl st into next ch, 1 dc into each of next 2 ch, 1 htr into each next 2 ch, 1 tr into each of next 2 ch, 1 dtr into each of next 3 ch. Join leaf to hat with a sl st into the front loop only of 4th st from beg of 12 ch, 1 sl st into the front loop of next st). Repeat from * 5 times.

3 Change to red and, working into the back loop of each st in the previous row, make 1 ch (1 dc into each of the next 5 sts, 2 dc into next st) 4 times, sl st into 1st dc at beg of round.

Round 8 1 ch (1 dc into each of next 6 sts, 2 dc in next st) 4 times, sl st into 1st dc.

Round 9 1 ch, (1 dc in each of next 7 sts, 2 dc into next st) 4 times, sl st into 1st dc.

Round 10 1 ch, (1 dc into each of next 8 sts, 2 dc into next st) 4 times, sl st into 1st dc.

Round 11 1 ch, (1 dc into each of next 9 sts, 2 dc into next st) 4 times, sl st into 1st dc.

Round 12 1 ch, (1 dc into each of 1st 10 sts, 2 dc into next st) 4 times, sl st into 1st dc.

Round 13 1 ch, 1 dc into each of 60 sts, sl st into 1st dc. Repeat round 13, 13 more times to row 27.

4 **Round 27** Change to 3.50mm hook and work 2 ch, 1 tr into same st, 1 tr into each of next 59 sts, sl st into 1st tr. Fasten off and sew in all ends of yarn.

5 If making the strawberry hat, embroider the seeds with black yarn. Work each one with a daisy stitch, keeping the floating threads between each stitch on the inside of the work as short as possible. Complete by making a small straight stitch in yellow in the centre of each black seed.

Cotton Duffle Bag

This lightweight duffle bag is made in natural unbleached crochet cotton. It can easily be packed away and would make an ideal beach bag for a summer holiday. Two different-sized hooks are used: a 3.50mm to make compact stitches for a firm base and a 4.50mm to achieve a bulkier crunchy effect for the openwork V-stitch sides. The two pieces are crocheted together to make a strong seam which will stand up to hard wear.

The finished bag measures 35cm (14in) deep and 51cm (20in) around the top.

MATERIALS
150g (5oz) craft cotton
3.50mm and 4.50mm crochet hooks
Tapestry needle

1 BASE With a 3.50mm hook, make 5 ch and join into a ring with a sl st into 1st ch.

Round 1 1 ch, 11 dc into ring, join with sl st to top of 1st ch (12 sts).

Round 2 3 ch (to stand as 1 tr), 1 tr into same place, (1 tr into next dc, 2 tr into next dc) to end of round, sl st to top of 3rd ch at beg of round (18 sts).

Round 3 3 ch, 1 tr into same place, 2 tr into each tr to end of round, sl st to top of 3rd ch (26 sts).

Round 4 3 ch, 1 tr into each tr to end of round, sl st to top of 3rd ch (54 sts).

Round 5 3 ch, (1 tr in each of next 2 tr, 2 tr in next tr), to end of round, sl st to top of 3rd ch (70 sts).

Round 6 3 ch, 1 tr into each tr, to end of round, sl st to top of 3rd ch (70 sts).

Round 7 3 ch, (1 tr into next tr, 2 tr into next tr) to end of round, sl st to top of 3rd ch (106 sts).

Round 8 3 ch, 1 tr in each tr to end of round, st st to top of 3 ch, finish off yarn (106 sts).

2 SIDES Using a 3.50mm hook, make 103 ch.

Row 1 1 tr into 4th ch from hook, 1 tr into each ch to end (100 tr), turn.

Row 2 3 ch (to stand as 1 tr), 1 tr into each tr to end (100 tr), turn.

Row 3 repeat row 2.

Row 4 Change to a 4.50mm hook.
4 ch, skip 2 tr (1 dtr, 1 ch, 1 dtr [= 1 V st] into next tr. miss 2 tr, 1 V st into next tr) to end of row, 1 dtr into last st, turn.

Row 5 4 ch (1 V st into 1 V st), repeat to end, 1 dtr into last st, (31 V sts), turn.

Rows 6–21 Repeat row 5, 16 times.

EYELET ROW Change to a 3.50mm hook.

Row 22 1 ch, 1 dc into each st of previous row (95 dc).

Row 23 1 ch, 1 dc into each dc to end (95 dc).

Row 24 3 ch, (1 tr into 1 dc) twice, (2 ch, skip 2 dc, 3 tr into next 3 dc) repeat to end of row, ending with 3 tr.

Row 25 1 ch, 1 dc into each st to end of row.

Row 26 1 ch, 1 dc into each dc to end of row. Finish off.

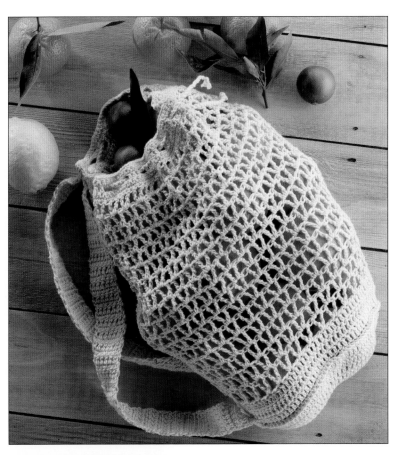

3 MAKING UP Press all the pieces lightly into shape and darn in any loose ends with a tapestry needle. Join the two short sides of the main bag together with double crochet, then attach the base in the same way to the lower edge of the bag.

SHOULDER STRAPS Using a 3.50mm hook, make 10 ch.
Row 1 make 1 tr in 4th ch from hook, 1 tr in each ch to end (7sts), turn.
Row 2 1 ch, 1 dc into each tr to end (7sts), turn.
Row 3 3 ch, 1 tr into each dc to end (7sts), turn.
Repeat rows 2 and 3 until the strap measures 51cm (20in).

4 Fold the strap in half and stitch securely to the top edge of the bag across the seam. Sew the two ends to the base of the bag as shown. Make a cord from a length of chain stitch or by twisting a long length of yarn back on itself, and thread through the eyelets.

Coasters and Placemat

Thick cotton in a subtle range of colours is used to crochet this placemat and coaster set, which makes it both attractive and practical; the yarn is heat-resistant, absorbent and keeps its shape when washed. The rectangular mat is in basketweave pattern. This raised-effect stitch is usually worked in a single colour, but the introduction of stripes gives it an added depth and texture. Making the coasters is a good way to practise crocheting circles; each is made in a different combination of three colours.

1 COASTERS
With colour 1, make 7 ch and join with sl st to form a circle.
Round 1 3 ch, 14 tr into circle, join with sl st into top of 3 ch.
Round 2 3 ch, 1 tr in same sp, (2 tr into 1 st) to end of round, join with sl st to top of 3 ch, break yarn (28 sts).

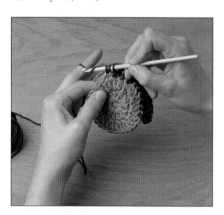

2 **Round 3** join colour 2. 3 ch, 1 tr (2 tr into next st, 1 tr) to end of round, join with sl st to top of 3 ch, break yarn (42 sts).
Round 4 join colour 3. 2 ch, 1 htr into each st to end of round, join with sl st to top of 2 ch (42 sts).

3 Finish off, darn in the end and press lightly.

COASTER MATERIALS
50g (2oz) balls of thick cotton yarn each in dark purple, claret, mustard, sage green and sap green
4.50mm crochet hook; large-eyed needle

1 PLACEMAT **Row 1** Using dark purple yarn, make 42 ch. Work 1 tr into 4th ch from hook, then 1 tr into each ch to end of row, turn.

Row 2 3 ch, yoh. Instead of working through loops at top of next tr, insert hook from right to left under the stitch itself, draw yarn through, then complete tr as usual (= 1 raised front treble, rftr). 1 rftr in next tr.

2 The next 3 raised sts are worked in the same way, but the hook is inserted from the back of the work and from right to left under the stitch (= raised back treble, rbtr). Work (3 rftr, 3 rbtr) 5 times to last 3 sts, 3 rftr, turn.

Row 3 3 ch, 2 rftr, (3 rbtr, 3 rftr) 6 times. Break yarn, turn.
Row 4 Join claret yarn and work 3 ch, 2 rftr (3 rbtr, 3 frtr) 6 times to end, turn.
Row 5 (3 rftr, 3 rbtr) 6 times to last 3 sts, 3 rftr, break yarn, turn.
These 2 rows form the basketweave pattern.
Continue working in the following stripes:
Rows 6 and 7 mustard
Rows 8 and 9 sage green
Rows 10 and 11 sap green
Rows 12 and 13 sage green
Rows 14 and 15 mustard
Rows 16 and 17 claret
Rows 18 to 20 dark purple.

3 Work the border in sage green. Join the yarn to the edge of the mat at the top right edge and work 1 tr in each st and 3 tr into each corner st. Along the sides, make 3 tr, evenly spaced, into the side of each tr, so that the stitches cover the loose ends of the yarn. Alternatively you can darn these in. Darn in the green yarn and press the mat lightly into shape.

PLACEMAT MATERIALS
50g (2oz) balls of thick cotton yarn each in dark purple, claret, mustard, sage green and sap green
4.00mm crochet hook; large-eyed needle

Curtain Heading

F ilet crochet is traditionally worked with a fine hook and white cotton thread and has always been a favourite trimming for net (lace) curtains and soft furnishings. This curtain heading is based on an Edwardian idea. It could be made with a full-length net or organza (organdy) curtain or as a shorter cafe-style curtain for a kitchen.

The lace could also be used as an insertion on linen and the lacets threaded with narrow ribbon. The border is 7.5cm (3in) deep and the repeat pattern measures 6.5cm (2½in).

MATERIALS
50g (2oz) ball of 20 crochet thread in white
1.25mm crochet hook
Sheer fabric measuring one and a half times the width
 of the window
Dressmaker's pins
White cotton sewing thread; needle
Brass curtain loops

1 Make 57 ch. **Row 1** 1 tr into 4th ch from hook, 1 tr into next tr, 2 ch, skip 2 ch, 1 dc into next ch, 2 ch, skip 2 ch, 1 tr into next ch, (2 ch, skip 2 ch, 1 tr into next ch) 6 times, 1 tr into each of next 3 ch (2 ch, skip 2 ch, 1 tr into next ch) 2 ch skip 2 ch, 1 dc into next ch, 2 ch, skip 2 ch, 1 tr into each of next 2 ch, turn.

Row 2 3 ch, 1 tr into 1 tr, 5 ch, 1 tr into next tr (2 ch, skip 2 ch, 1 tr into next tr) 5 times, 2 tr into sp, 1 tr into next tr, 11 ch, skip 2 tr, 1 tr into next tr, 2 tr into sp, (2 ch, skip 2 ch, 1 tr into next tr) 5 times, 5 ch, 1 tr into each of next 2 tr, turn.

Row 3 3 ch, tr into 1 tr, 2 ch, skip 2 ch, 1 dc into next ch, 2 ch, skip 2 ch, 1 tr into next tr (lacet st made) (2 ch, skip 2 ch, 1 tr into next tr) 4 times, 2 tr into sp, 1 tr into next tr, 6 ch, 3 dc into 11 ch loop, 6 ch, skip 3 tr, 1 tr into next tr, 2 tr into sp, 1 tr into next tr (2 ch, skip 2 ch, 1 tr into next tr) 4 times, 2 ch, skip 2 ch, 1 dc into next ch, 2 ch, skip 2 ch, 1 tr into each of next 2 tr, turn.

Row 4 3 ch, 1 tr into next tr, 5 ch, 1 tr into next tr (2 ch, skip 2 ch, 1 tr into next tr) 3 times, 2 tr into next sp, 1 tr into next tr, 6 ch, 1 dc into sp, 1 dc into each of next 3 dc, 1 dc into sp, 6 ch, skip next 3 tr, 1 tr into 4th tr, 2 tr into next sp, 1 tr into next tr (2 ch, skip 2 ch, 1 tr into next tr) 3 times, 5 ch, 1 tr into each of next 2 tr, turn.

Row 5 3 ch, 1 tr into next tr, 2 ch, skip 2 ch, 1 dc into next ch, 2 ch, skip 2 ch, 1 tr into next tr, (2 ch, skip 2 ch, 1 tr) twice, 2 tr into next sp, 1 tr into next tr, 6 ch, 1 dc into sp, 1 dc into each of next 5 dc, 1 dc into sp, 6 ch, skip 3 tr, 1 tr into next tr, 2 tr into sp, 1 tr into next tr, (2 ch, skip 2 ch, 1 tr into next tr) twice, 2 ch, skip 2 ch, 1 dc into next ch, 2 ch, skip 2 ch, 1 tr into each of next 2 tr, turn.

Row 6 3 ch, 1 tr into next tr, 5 ch, 1 tr into next tr, 2 ch, skip 2 ch, 1 tr into next tr, 2 tr into sp, 1 tr into next tr, 6 ch, 1 dc into sp, 1 dc into each of next 7 dc, 1 dc into sp, 6 ch, skip 3 tr, 1 tr into next tr, 2 tr into next sp, 1 tr into 1 tr, 2 ch, skip 2 ch, 1 tr into next tr, 5 ch, 1 tr into each of next 2 tr, turn.

Row 7 3 ch, 1 tr into next tr, 2 ch, skip 2 ch, 1 dc into next ch, 2 ch, skip 2 ch, 1 tr into next tr, 2 ch, skip 2 ch, 1 tr into next tr, 2 ch, skip 2 tr, 1 tr into next tr, 3 tr into sp, 6 ch, skip 1 dc, 1 dc into each of next 7 dc, 6 ch, 3 tr into sp, 1 tr into next tr, skip 2 tr, 1 tr into next tr, 2 ch skip 2 ch, 1 tr into next tr, 2 ch, skip 2 ch, 1 dc into next ch, 2 ch, skip 2 ch, 1 tr into each of next 2 tr, turn.

Row 8 3 ch, 1 tr into next tr, 5 ch, 1 tr into next tr, (2ch, skip 2 ch, 1 tr into next tr) twice, 2 ch, skip 2 tr, 1 tr into next tr, 3 tr into sp, 6 ch, skip 1 dc, 1 dc into each of next 5 dc, 6 ch, 3 tr into sp, 1 tr into next tr, 2 ch, skip 2 tr, 1 tr into next tr (2 ch, skip 2 ch, 1 tr into next tr) twice, 5 ch, 1 tr into each of next 2 tr, turn.

Row 9 3 ch, 1 tr into next tr, 2 ch, skip 2 ch, 1 dc into next ch, 2 ch, skip 2 ch, 1 tr into next tr (2ch, skip 2 ch, 1 tr into next tr) 3 times, 2 ch, skip 2 tr, 1 tr into next tr, 3 tr into sp, 5 ch, skip 1 dc, 1 dc into each of next 3 dc, 5 ch, 3 tr into sp, 1 tr into next tr, 2 ch, skip 2 tr, 1 tr into next tr, (2 ch, skip 2 ch, 1 tr into next tr) 3 times, 2 ch, skip 2 ch, 1 dc into next ch, skip 2 ch, 1 tr into each of next 2 tr, turn.

2 **Row 10** 3 ch, 1 tr into next tr, 5 ch, 1 tr into next tr, (2 ch, skip 2 ch, 1 tr into next tr) 4 times, 2 ch, skip 2 tr, 1 tr into next tr, 3 tr into sp, 2 ch, 3 tr into sp, 1 tr into next tr, 2 ch, skip 2 tr, 1 tr into next tr, (2 ch, skip 2 ch, 1 tr into next tr) 4 times, 5 ch, 1 tr into each of next 2 tr, turn.

Row 11 3 ch, 1 tr into next tr, 2 ch, skip 2 ch, 1 dc into next ch, 2 ch, skip 2 ch, 1 tr into next tr, (2 ch, skip 2 ch, 1 tr into next tr) 5 times, 2 ch, skip 2 tr, 1 tr into next tr, 2 tr into 2 ch sp, 1 tr into next tr (2 ch, skip 2ch, 1 tr into next tr) 6 times, 2 ch, skip 2 ch, 1 dc into next ch, 2 ch, 1 tr into each of next 2 tr.

These 11 rows form the pattern: work the length to fit the window where the curtain is to be hung. Sew the ends and press lightly.

3 TO MAKE UP Hem the fabric around all four sides and sew a line of loose running stitch along the top edge. Draw up the thread.

4 Pin the fabric to the lace and adjust the gathers to fit. Stitch the two edges together tidily.

5 Sew the loops to the top of the curtain, spacing them evenly.

Jug (Pitcher) Cover

L acy beaded jug (pitcher) covers were popular in Victorian times, both indoors, where they were used to protect the milk in the pantry or on the tea table, and outside, where they were a vital summer picnic accessory, keeping insects away from lemonade. This pretty modern version is crocheted in fine blue and white thread and edged with brightly coloured, clear glass beads.

MATERIALS

*20g (³⁄₄oz) ball of 20 crochet thread in white and a
  small quantity in blue*
1.25mm crochet hook; 28 glass beads

INSTRUCTIONS

Using blue thread, make 10 ch, sl st to form a circle.
Round 1 into circle make: 4 ch, 4 dtr. Remove hook, insert into top of 4 ch and then into top of 4th dtr. yoh (yo) and draw through to form popcorn st, 6 ch *(5dtr into circle, remove hook, insert into top of 1st dtr, then into top of 5th dtr, yoh, draw through to form popcorn st, 6 ch). Repeat from * 5 times, 6 popcorn sts made, sl st to top of 1st popcorn st. Finish off blue thread.
Round 2 join white thread to centre of any 6 ch loop. 7 ch, *into next loop make 3 dtr leaving last loop of each st on hook, yoh, draw through all loops on hook – 1 dtr cluster made – 7 ch. Into same loop make (1 dtr cluster, 7 ch) twice. Repeat from * twice, 1 dc into next 6 ch loop, sl st to 1st ch made.
Round 3 sl st along 1st 4 ch of next 7 ch loop *9 ch, 1 dc into next 7 ch loop. Repeat from * to end of round, sl st to 1st ch.
Round 4 sl st along 5 ch of next 9 ch loop *11 ch, 1 dc into next 9 ch loop. Repeat from * to end of round, sl st to 1st ch made.
Round 5 sl st along next 6 ch *13 ch. 1 dc into next 11 ch loop. Repeat from * to end of round, sl st to 1st ch made.
Round 6 sl st along 7 ch. 9 ch, *(1 dtr cluster, 7 ch) three times, 1 dtr cluster, 9 ch, 1 dc into next loop. Repeat from * five times, sl st to 1st ch made.
Round 7 sl st along 5 ch *(7 ch, 1 dc into next loop). Repeat from * to end of round, sl st to 1st ch. Fasten off white thread.
Round 8 join blue thread to 4th ch of any 7 ch loop. *(3 ch, 1 tr, 2 ch, 2 tr) all into same ch sp, 1 ch (2 tr, 2 ch, 2 tr) into centre ch of next loop, 1 ch. Repeat from * to end of round, sl st to 1st ch.
Round 9 1 sl st into next tr, sl st into next 2 ch sp (3 ch, 2 tr, 3 ch, 3 tr) all into 2 ch sp. 1 dc into next 1 ch sp. Into next 2

ch sp make *(3 tr, 3 ch, 3 tr, 1 dc into 1 ch sp). Repeat from * to end of round, sl st to top of 1st 3 ch. Finish off blue thread.
Round 10 rejoin white thread to a 4 ch sp behind blue shell, working into the last white row. (7 ch, 1 dc into next 4th ch) to end, sl st to 1st ch.
Round 11 sl st to 4th ch of loop. (9 ch, 1 dc into next loop) to end, sl st to 1st ch.
Round 12 sl st along 5 ch (11 ch, 1 dc into next loop) to end, sl st to 1st ch.
Round 13 repeat round 12.
Round 14 repeat round 12.
Round 15 sl st to 6th ch (12 ch, 1 dc into next loop) to end, sl st to 1st ch.
Round 16 repeat row 15.
Round 17 sl st to 6th ch (13 ch, 1 dc into next loop) to end, sl st to 1st ch.
Round 18 sl st to 7th ch (14 ch, 1 dc into next loop) to end, sl st to 1st ch.
Round 19 from the ball in use measure a length of yarn about 4.5m (5yd) long and cut. Thread the beads on to the yarn.

ATTACHING THE BEADS
*(14 ch, remove hook from loop. Slip one bead over chain, put hook back into loop, 1 dc into next loop). Repeat from * to end, sl st to 1st ch. Fasten off and tidy ends. Press lightly.

Snowflake Motif

Crochet motifs can be used in a great variety of ways. The appearance of one basic shape can be changed if it is worked in different colours and various weights of thread. This six-sided pattern can be made singly or several can either be joined together to make a mat or, for the ambitious, a table cloth.

MATERIALS
Small quantity of 20 crochet thread
1.25mm crochet hook
Pearl beads (optional)

Make 12 ch and join into a ring with sl st into 1st ch.
Round 1 3 ch, into ring make 2 tr, 5 ch, (3 tr, 5 ch) 5 times, sl st to top of 3rd ch at beg of round (6 sp).

1 Round 2 sl st to 5 ch sp. 4 ch, 4 tr, 4 ch, 5 tr *into next sp make (5 tr, 4 ch, 5 tr). Repeat from * 5 times, sl st to 4th ch.

2 Round 3 sl st to next 4 ch sp, 3 ch, 3 tr, 3 ch, 4 tr, 3 ch * into next sp make (4 tr, 3 ch, 4 tr, 3 ch). Repeat from * 5 times, sl st to 4th ch.

Round 4 sl st to next sp. (3 ch, 2 tr, 3 ch, 3 tr) into sp, 6 ch, 1 dc into next 3 ch sp, 6 ch, *(3 tr, 3 ch, 3 tr into next 4 ch sp, 6 ch,1 dc into 3 ch sp, 6 ch). Repeat from * 5 times, sl st to 3rd ch.
Round 5 sl st to 3 ch loop, (3 ch, 1 tr, 3 ch, 2 tr) into 3 ch sp. 6 ch, 1 dc into 6 ch sp, 3 ch, 1 dc into 6 ch sp, 6 ch *(2 tr, 3 ch, 2 tr all into 3 ch sp, 6 ch, 1 dc into 6 ch sp, 3 ch, 1 dc into 6 ch sp). Repeat from * 5 times, sl st to 2nd ch.

3 Finish off and darn in the loose ends. Pin out to shape on a cloth, pulling out the six points of the star, and press lightly with a damp cloth.

4 Just the first two rounds can be crocheted to make a tiny motif, which fits perfectly into a brooch mount.

Special Techniques

This section is an introduction to the many needlework techniques which fall outside the usual categories. Some, like smocking and rug-making, are crafts in themselves, whilst others will provide innovative ideas to add an individual touch to your projects. Familiar items such as beads, sequins, tassels, ribbons and buttons can all be used in creative and sometimes unexpected ways – all that is needed is a little ingenuity!

Dyeing

Using dyes to bring original colours to yarn and cloth can add a whole new dimension to many textile crafts. Traditional vegetable dyeing techniques give subtle and sometimes unexpected hues, and using them is an art in itself. Chemical dyes, however, are straightforward and quick to use, and are available in both hot- and cold-water versions for synthetic and natural fibres. Special compounds that can be used safely in the washing machine are suitable for larger quantities of material.

SPACE-DYED YARNS

Hanks of cotton thread or pure wool can be dyed as easily as fabrics, with exciting results. The random colour bands that are formed by space-dyeing yarn will create interesting patterns when the threads are worked up. Finer threads can be dyed for free-form embroidery stitches, in specially chosen co-ordinating colours.

1 Wind the yarn into hanks and secure at intervals. Loose ties will allow the colours to blend gently; tight ties will leave a resist band of white yarn. Soak well, then wring out excess water.

2 Following the manufacturer's instructions, prepare the hot-water dye solution in an old saucepan and maintain it at simmering point. When working with several dyes, only a small amount of each powder need be used. Holding the yarn with a pair of tongs, dip the parts of the skein in between the ties into the dye for a minute. Repeat with the second and third colours.

3 Wash the skeins in a hand-wash liquid to remove any surplus dye, rinse well and allow to dry thoroughly. Carefully snip away the ties without cutting through the yarn, then wind into balls.

It is fascinating to knit or crochet with space-dyed yarns and watch the haphazard colours fall into orderly diamonds and stripes.

Carefully planned space-dyeing is used to produce the figurative and geometric design that patterns the warp of this decorative Ikat fabric.

Tie-Dye Scarf

Tie-dyeing is a well-known way of producing surface patterns on fabric or garments, and, perhaps because of this overfamiliarity, it is often underestimated. Simply knotting, gathering, folding or pleating the material and tying it with string, or binding it with elastic bands, will create varied and unpredictable shapes. Several colours can be used on one piece for a vivid multicoloured effect.

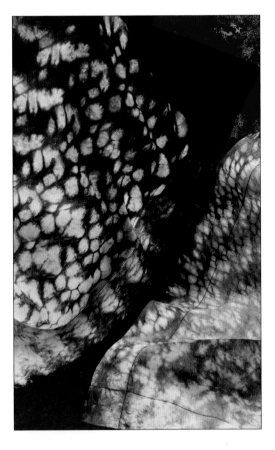

MATERIALS
Large scarf in plain white silk or cotton
String
Hot- or cold-water dye
Salt

VARIATION 1
Circular designs are created by placing a bead or button in the centre of the fabric and holding it in place with an elastic band. Bunch the rest of the material together and tie it at intervals with string.

VARIATION 2
Roll or fold the fabric into a roll and bind at random for a striped effect.

1 If the scarf is new, wash it to remove any dressing (finishing). Rinse well, then wring out. Lay it out on a flat surface and place a long piece of string over one corner. Carefully roll the fabric over the string.

2 Pull the two ends of the string together, gently easing the fabric into a circular shape and making sure that it does not unravel. Knot the string securely.

3 Dye the scarf, following the manufacturer's instructions, and using an old saucepan as a dyebath. Cut the string and unroll the fabric. Wash again to remove any surplus dye.

225

Fabric-Strip Rugs

A hand-made hearth rug in front of the fireplace has long been a feature of family life. Scraps of wool and fabric can be stitched or tufted on to a backing cloth or canvas to form elaborate pictorial designs, but the quickest rugmaking methods are those in which the rug itself is constructed from strips of braided fabric.

BRAIDED RUGS

Braided rugs, which are made from a coiled stitched braid of material, are among some of the oldest surviving antique examples. This technique was often used in combination with knitting, particularly by the Amish people of Lancaster County, Pennsylvania. A central medallion, made from fabric knitted into squares or six-pointed stars, would be surrounded by braided bands. If possible, cut the fabric strips on the diagonal so they will be less rigid. Cloth salvaged from women's and girls' dresses was cut into long strips, then joined and wound into a ball for working. Knitting with fabric strips can be hard work since they have no elasticity. It is important to keep the tension quite loose and to work on extra-large needles – size 10.00mm upwards.

1 MAKING A KNITTED RUG Collect together scraps and remnants of patterned dress-weight fabrics and tear into 4cm (1½in) strips. Sew together and wind into a ball.

2 The rug is knitted in strips of approximately 7.5cm (3in) wide, as anything else would be too unwieldy. Cast on 10 stitches and work in garter stitch as usual. This will make the rug reversible.

3 The finished strips can be sewn together with strong thread. By working in strips of even length, you can produce a chequered (checkered) pattern.

This crochet rug has been worked in basic double crochet stitch with a 12.00mm hook. Each round is worked in a separate colour to give a pattern of concentric circles and the soft colours come from using old fabric.

Braided Rug

The first fabric-strip floorcoverings were made at a time when new cloth was in short supply. Their distinctive muted appearance came from the use of mixed fabrics, recycled from clothing and domestic textiles, as few of the early makers could afford the luxury of planning a special colour scheme for their work. The striking effect of this round rug shows how a traditional technique can be updated to create an unquestionably modern effect. It is made from a vivid selection of bright acetate fabrics, overdyed ginghams and sari fabric.

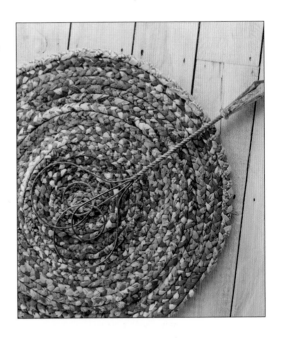

MATERIALS
Selection of coloured fabrics
Button-hole thread
Sewing needle
Safety pin
Kitchen weights (optional)
Heavy-duty fabric for the backing (optional)

1 Tear the fabric, along the grain, into strips that measure about 6.5m (2½in) wide. Three strips of the same shade braided together will give a broad strip of colour, whereas mixing the colours will produce a "speckled" effect.

2 Stitch three strips together at one end, then secure to a firm surface: fasten to the arm of an upholstered chair with a safety pin, hold down with large kitchen weights, or attach to a wall hook.

3 Plait (braid) the three strips together, turning the raw edges to the inside. Further lengths can either be stitched on, end to end, as the plait progresses, or folded around the end of the preceding strip as shown, to save time sewing.

4 When the braid is a few metres (yards) long, the sewing process can begin. Tidy the stitched end, then, working on a flat surface, coil the braid around it. Sew together with ladder stitch or a flat stitch, catching together a small amount of fabric from each side, and turning to maintain a round shape. A strip of about 18m (20yd) will make a circle of 60cm (24in) diameter, and the rug can be enlarged to any size. A heavy-duty backing fabric can be sewn on if the rug is to receive a lot of wear.

Smocking

Smocking has been used in garment making, as an ornamental method of gathering surplus material, since medieval times. In the English countryside, smock frocks were worn by male agricultural workers for centuries and the tradition survived in rural Essex among the older generation until the 1930s. The smock was a practical, protective, outer garment made from tough linen that could stand up to heavy wear and repel water. It was made from large rectangles of fabric with the fullness gathered into narrow pleats at the yoke, shoulders and cuffs and held together with rows of smocking stitches.

HOW TO WORK SMOCKING

Before being embroidered, the fabric must be drawn into narrow tubes. Rows of dots, in a grid formation, are marked on the reverse of the fabric. Iron-on transfers are the quickest way to prepare plain or patterned fabric.

1 Place the transfer face down and press carefully. Work a row of gathering stitches from right to left, along each horizontal line, picking up a few threads at each dot.

2 Pull all the lengths of cotton up evenly, so that the fabric falls into a series of tubes. Secure the ends by tying them.

3 You can gather fabrics printed with regular dots or checks by simply following the lines of the pattern.

HONEYCOMB STITCH

This is worked along two rows of dots. Bring the needle out to the left of the first fold and work two back stitches over the first two folds. Bring the needle down and out on the next row of dots, between the next two folds. Work two back stitches over these and bring the needle back up to the top line of stitches. Continue to the end of the row, then work the next line of stitches on the third and fourth rows of dots. Surface honeycomb stitch is worked in the same way, but the needle is passed over the surface of the fabric, rather than through the tube.

CABLE STITCH

This stitch is also worked from left to right. Start at the left of the first fold. Be sure that the thread lies below the needle. Make a stitch over the second fold and bring the needle out between the first two folds. Hold the thread above the needle and make a stitch over the third fold, bringing the needle out between the second and third fold. Continue to the end.

Child's Sun Dress

The appealing charm of smocking has made it a favourite for children's clothes, and generations of young girls have worn floral print frocks with smocked yokes. This pretty sun dress would fit a toddler of up to eighteen months, and requires only the most basic of dressmaking skills. The bodice is worked in honeycomb stitch, which produces a very elastic fabric that eliminates the need for a back opening or any fastening.

MATERIALS
35 x 154cm (14 x 60in) piece of dotted cotton fabric
Matching cotton sewing thread; sewing machine
Cotton tacking (basting) thread; needle; dressmaker's pins
Stranded embroidery thread in blue, blue-green,
   green, pale blue-green, white, pale lime green,
   yellow and bright yellow

1 Cut a strip of fabric measuring 30 x 154cm (12 x 60in). Turn in a narrow hem at the top and bottom edges, machine stitch and trim back. Turn over and machine again.

2 On the wrong side of the fabric, work six long rows of contrasting gathering thread, starting about 2cm (¾in) in from one hemmed edge. Use the printed dots as a guide, but if they are too far apart, pick up a few threads of cloth between each one.

3 Draw up the gathers and secure by wrapping thread round pins. On the right side of the fabric, beginning at the outside edge of the gathers, work eight rows of surface honey-comb stitch in colours as follows: blue, blue-green, green, pale blue-green, white, pale lime green, yellow and bright yellow. Remove the gathering stitches and machine stitch the back seam. Tidy with zigzag stitch and trim.

4 Cut four strips of fabric each measuring 5 x 30cm (2 x 12in) to make the straps. Fold with right sides together and machine stitch, tapering off at one end. Trim and turn through. Press, top stitch and tidy the raw end. Sew the straps securely to the inside of the yoke at the top of the stitching. Finish off by knotting together at the shoulders.

Ribbons and Bows

There are many craft applications for ribbons, which are available in an ever-increasing choice of weights, patterns and widths. Manufacturers are constantly developing new ideas, such as sheer rainbow gauzes, metallic gold and silver braids (which are ideal for Christmas decorations) and reversible printed satin ribbons. More traditional types – moiré taffeta, country-style ginghams, luxurious velvets and grosgrain – can be found in a wide range of colours in craft shops and department stores.

RIBBON ROSES, ROSETTES, BOWS AND FAVOURS

These can be used to add a personal touch to all kinds of gifts and accessories. Special Valentine ribbons printed with hearts, Christmas designs or wedding ribbons with a pattern of bells and lucky horseshoes can all be used to decorate special presents. Look out for pastel baby ribbons to decorate tiny garments or blankets. Lengths of ribbon can also be appliquéd on to a fabric background.

Ribbon roses are suprisingly straightforward to make and can be used to decorate many different sewing projects. Satin ribbons give a luxurious effect, especially if several harmonizing colours are used together.

1 RIBBON ROSE
Fold the ribbon under at a right angle, two-thirds along its length, and then pass the long end under the triangular fold and hold in place. Pass the short end under, then continue to make accordion folds to the end of the ribbon.

2 Hold the two ends together and grip with the thumb and forefinger of one hand while drawing up the long end. This action ruffles the ribbon and forms the rose.

3 Still holding the rose, so that it does not come undone, stitch through the base to hold the petals in place.

WIRE-EDGED RIBBONS
These make spectacular bows, which will retain their shape. The loops and ends can be gently bent into flowing curves.

Ribbon-Weave Cushion (Pillow)

Authentic tartan (plaid) and textured grosgrain ribbons are woven together to make this eye-catching cushion (pillow). The basic technique used is called a square (or tabby) weave. The foundation ribbons are laid down to form the warp, then further lengths of ribbon, known as the weft, are passed alternately under and over them. Endless variations can be produced, by using different colours and widths of ribbon in various combinations.

1 Place the bonding web shiny side down on a clean, flat surface. Cut the ribbon into 30.5cm (12in) lengths. There should be 26 lengths altogether. Arrange single lengths of ribbon across the web in the order: B, E, A, C, D, B, F, B, D, C, A, E, B. Pin each end of the ribbons to the web.

2 Weave the remaining ribbons vertically through the horizontal lengths in the same order. Pin them at each end in the same way to hold them in place. You should end up with an exact 30.5cm (12in) square.

3 To adhere the ribbon to the fusible bonding web, place a sheet of baking parchment over the ribbons (to protect the iron plate), and use the heat of the iron to bond the layers together. Press from the centre out and remove the pins as you come to them, rather than ironing over them. Follow the manufacturer's instructions as a guide to pressing time.

Materials

A: 122cm (48in) length of red tartan (plaid) ribbon 4cm (1¹/₂in) wide
B: 244cm (96in) length of blue tartan (plaid) ribbon 2.5cm (1in) wide
C: 122cm (48in) length of green ribbon 2.5cm (1in) wide
D: 122cm (48in) length of red ribbon 1cm (³/₈in) wide
E: 122cm (48in) length of blue ribbon 1cm (³/₈in) wide
F: 61cm (24in) length of yellow ribbon 2.5cm (1in) wide
Masking tape
30.5cm (12in) square, at least, of fusible bonding web
Two x 30.5cm (12in) squares of backing fabric
28cm (11in) square cushion (pillow) pad
Sewing machine; machine sewing thread to match the ribbon and/or backing fabric; iron; pins; and baking parchment

4 Remove the parchment and check that the ribbon is firmly adhered. Trim away any excess web. Remove the shiny backing paper from the other side of the fusible web and place the ribbon panel web side down on to a backing square. This layer won't be seen, but will provide stability to the ribbon weave, so it can be quite a thin fabric. Fuse the fabrics together as before, protecting the ironing board and iron from the glue. Stitch around the edge of the panel to secure the layers together.

5 To make up the cushion, place the cushion backing and the ribbon panel right sides together. Pin, then machine stitch around the cushion leaving a large gap in one side. Turn the cushion through to the right side, push out the corners and press. Insert the cushion pad, then slip stitch the gap closed.

Tassels and Pompoms

A whole art surrounds the making of furnishing trimmings, which is correctly known as *passementerie*, and the most elaborate tassels and fringes can be very expensive. The basic shapes are not difficult to make, however, and a special tassel can add a distinctive finishing touch to many projects. Virtually any yarn or thread can be used: raffia gives a natural feel to bedroom and bathroom accessories, gold machine embroidery thread is extravagant enough for the most special gifts, chenille yarn is luxurious, while bright wools or cotton yarns create a less sophisticated effect. Tassels can be made to coordinate with any interior design scheme and to adorn most soft furnishings.

HOW TO MAKE A TASSEL

Different weights of yarn will produce different results, but the basic method does not vary. The top of the tassel can be further ornamented with a binding of contrasting threads or by the addition of beads.

1 Cut a piece of cardboard slightly wider than the finished tassel and wind the thread around it. Tie a length of thread around the loop when it has reached the required thickness.

2 Slip the loop from the cardboard, hold the tied end firmly and cut through the threads at the opposite end.

3 Keep the tassel in shape by binding the top with matching thread and finishing off the ends securely.

BLACK VELVET AND CHENILLE YARN

Opulent velvet and chenille yarn have been combined to make this spectacular cushion (pillow) above. The blue tassels are sewn by hand at regular intervals and contrast with the smooth texture of the velvet cover.

Pompom Necklace

Like tassels, pompoms are easy and fun to make, especially for children. They can be used to decorate hats, scarves and sweaters, strung together to make soft toys – caterpillars or snakes – or threaded with beads to make this colourful play necklace. These pompoms are all made from a single colour of cotton yarn, which has a rich velvety finish, but interesting multicoloured effects can be produced by mixing yarns.

MATERIALS
Pair of compasses; pencil
Cardboard
Darning needle
Remnants of cotton yarn in various colours
Round cord elastic
Multicoloured wooden beads

1 Using the compasses, draw two 4cm (1½in) circles on the cardboard and mark 2cm (¾in) circles within them. Cut out round the outer card and inner circles to form the two cardboard rings. Thread the darning needle with yarn and, holding the two cardboard rings together, begin to wrap the yarn around the cardboard as shown.

2 Continue until the cardboard is completely covered and the centre space filled, adding extra yarn as necessary. Cut carefully around the outside edge, inserting the scissor blades between the discs.

3 Wrap a length of yarn several times around the cut strands, and between the cardboard discs. Tie loosely in a knot, then remove the cardboard discs. Trim the pompom to make a tidy round ball. Make seven more pompoms in the same way, using different colours.

4 Thread the needle with elastic and string on three wooden beads. Push the needle through the centre of the first pompom, then add another three beads.

Continue until all the elements have been threaded together, then tie the elastic tightly in a knot and hide the ends by threading them back through the beads.

Beads and Sequins

Embroidery with beads and sequins has always been associated with glamorous fashion garments – from the fantasy wedding dresses that provide the finale to Paris fashion shows, to the eleborate confections worn by ballroom dancers. A more restrained use of beading can bring interest to many textile techniques, by highlighting detail and adding colour.

WORKING WITH BEADS AND SEQUINS

Sequins can be bought from many craft suppliers. Some of the most exciting varieties are imported from India and come in exotic shapes and colours. They can be sewn on in three ways: in overlapping rows so that the thread is hidden; with decorative contrasting stitches; or anchored in place with a small bead.

FLOWER SEQUINS
Tiny white rocaille beads will make attractive ornamental centres for these flower-shaped sequins.

SEWING A ROW OF SEQUINS
Bring the needle through a sequin's centre hole and make a straight stitch over the edge. Place the edge of the next sequin over the hole in the first. Bring the needle up through its centre and sew down, over the edge.

SEWING ON BEADS
Individual beads can be sewn into elaborate patterns: stitch each one down with a fine needle.

CONTINUOUS THREAD
Using decorative back stitches, so that the thread can be seen through the fabric, gold sequins have been sewn on to metallic organza (organdy).

FLAT SEQUINS
Using a fine needle, thread through both the sequin and a bead, then take the thread back through the hole so that the sequin is held in place by the bead.

CUP SEQUINS
This star-shaped Indian Christmas decoration is covered in glittering muticoloured cup sequins, held down by small iridescent beads.

Lace edgings can be decorated with beads and sequins to emphasize aspects of the woven design.

Once part of a chair seat cover, this hydrangea-like flower is made up entirely of beads that have been stitched on to double-thread canvas.

Beaded Heart

Silk flowers and fine satin ribbons combine with beads and sequins to lend an Edwardian appearance to this romantic heart. It is based on a piece of antique lace that has been given a new lease of life: the damaged areas have been disguised with cut-out motifs and beading, and the fragile fabric tacked (basted) on to a heart-shaped padded cushion (pillow) as support. The finished heart would look lovely on a dressing-table, but could also be hung in a wardrobe to perfume clothes.

MATERIALS
Satin fabric
Matching sewing thread
Polyester toy stuffing
Potpourri (optional)
Fragment of old lace
Tiny glass beads
Translucent sequins
Dressmaker's pins
Silk flowers and leaves
Narrow ribbon

1 Cut out two heart shapes from the satin and, with right sides facing, stitch together, leaving a small space in one side. Clip the curves and corners and turn through. Fill with toy stuffing and slip stitch the opening together. Potpourri could be added to give a sweet scent.

2 Mark out the heart shape on the lace, then sew it with beads and sequins, picking out the shapes within the lace pattern. Cut out small motifs from the spare pieces of lace to cover any holes.

3 Pin the lace on to the heart cushion (pillow), stretching it over the upper part and folding over the surplus fabric. Stitch in place, then sew on a posy of silk flowers and ribbons.

235

Buttons

Buttons are essentially a utilitarian part of everyday life, used by everybody to do up their clothing. Over the years they have been made from every imaginable material: horn, seashell, coconut, plastic, glass, pottery and metal. Elaborate buttons have always been a fashion accessory in themselves. Eighteenth-century dandies sported buttons of gold set with semi-precious stones or even painted with miniature portraits. Today the interlocking Cs on a Chanel suit are instantly recognizable and say as much about the wearer as monogrammed blazer buttons.

SELF-COVER BUTTONS

Fabric-covered buttons are used by dressmakers as an unobtrusive yet decorative fastening. Larger version are used for soft furnishings to match or contrast with upholstery fabric, but can also be covered with small circles of embroidery or needlepoint.

This fascinating set of buttons was made as showcase for various specialized stitches and includes blackwork, drawn threadwork, needleweaving, laid threadwork and inlay appliqué.

1 Following the manufacturer's guide, which is supplied with self-cover button kit, cut out a circle of fabric to fit the button top.

2 Run a gathering thread around the edge of the fabric, draw up and slip over the button top. Pull tightly and secure, then press the backing firmly into place.

Buttons can be combined with many embroidery and applique techniques. Mother-of-pearl shirt buttons have been stitched to the centres of these cotton flowers and are well suited to the naive graphic style of the piece.

Button Mirror

In addition to their obvious function, buttons can be put to many decorative uses. This mirror frame is ornamented with simple embroidery stitches, tiny discs of Indian shisha glass and round mother-of-pearl buttons. Raid the button box to find a selection of buttons in various shapes, colours and sizes; this monochrome colour scheme is just one interpretation of the idea.

MATERIALS
Dressmaker's chalk or carbon
Piece of black cotton twill 5cm (2in)
  larger all round than the frame
Wooden frame 5cm (2in) wide
Mother-of-pearl buttons
Embroidery thread in red and silver
Shisha glass
Pva adhesive
Buttonhole thread
Mirror to fit inside the frame
Panel pins

1 Draw the outline on to the fabric, using the frame as a template. Mark on the positions of the two rows of shisha glass, buttons and crosses. Sew on the buttons, using red or silver thread, and glue on the shisha glass with pva adhesive.

2 Embroider the crosses in silver thread. The arrangement of shisha, buttons and crosses should not be too orderly or regular. Cut out the centre rectangle of fabric, leaving an allowance of at least 2.5cm (1in).

3 Stretch the fabric over the frame and fold over the edges. Draw together with large stitches in buttonhole thread. Mitre the outside corners and neatly finish the inside corners. Fix the mirror securely in place with panel pins.

Templates

This section gives all the patterns, charts and templates needed for making the step-by-step projects. Many of them have been reduced and can be increased to the size required by using a photocopier. Alternatively, the grid outlines can be used as a guide for enlarging by hand.

To enlarge the patterns shown on grids, find or draw onto paper a grid of 1in (25mm) squares. Taking one square at a time, copy the lines of the pattern onto your full-size grid. This will give an actual-size pattern.

Embroidery – Alphabet Sampler

Embroidery – Cross Stitch Motifs

GARLAND

WOVEN HEART

LITTLE SCHOOLHOUSE

VALENTINE HEART AND BOW

SCANDINAVIAN HEART

Embroidery – Potpourri Bag

Embroidery – Fabric Book

Embroidery – Tea Towel

Embroidery –
House and Garden Picture

Embroidery – Rocket Bag

Embroidery – Folk Art Gloves

Embroidery – Hairslide (Barrette)

Embroidered – Hat

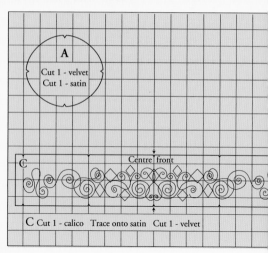

Embroidery – Picture Frame

Embroidery – Drawstring Bag

Embroidery – Placemat

B

Cut 1 - velvet
Cut 1 - satin

CM (5/8IN) SEAM ALLOWANCE INCLUDED

A

b
b
a
b

b

Embroidery – Cat Picture

Embroidery – Fish Mobile

Embroidery – Table Cloth

Needlepoint – Jewellery Box

Needlepoint – Lone-star Cushion (Pillow)

	Pale lilac		Light turquoise		Dark peach
	Dark purple		Crimson		Orange
	Indigo		Dark turquoise		Dark gold

Needlepoint – Nine-star Cushion (Pillow)

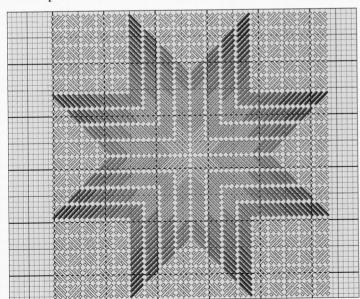

	Pale lemon
	Light gold
	Pale pink
	Dark pink
	Dark gold
	Rust
	Burgundy
	Cream

Needlepoint – Heart Picture

Needlepoint – Circular Star

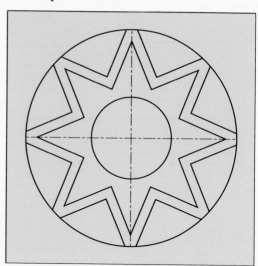

Needlepoint – Cup and Saucer

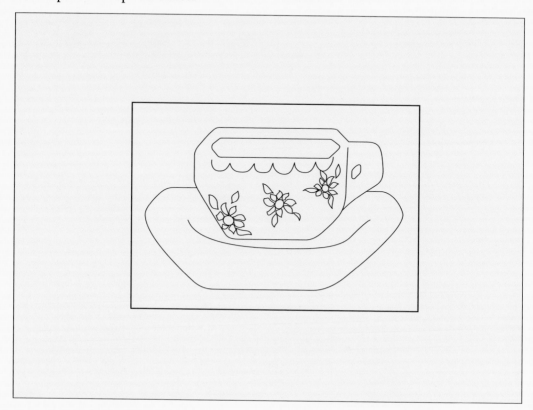

Needlepoint – Sun Pincushion

Needlepoint – Brooch Cushion (Pillow)

	White
	Pale blue
	Mid-blue
	Dark blue
	Indigo

Needlepoint – Needle Book

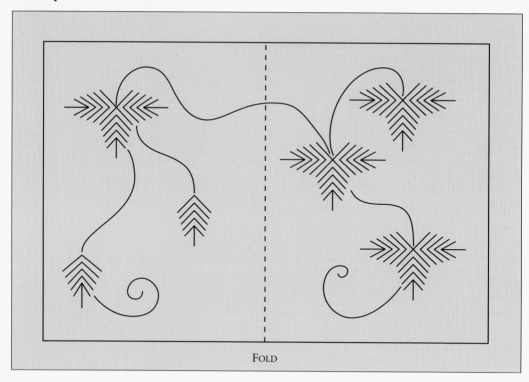

FOLD

Needlepoint – Scissor Case

Patchwork – Red Star

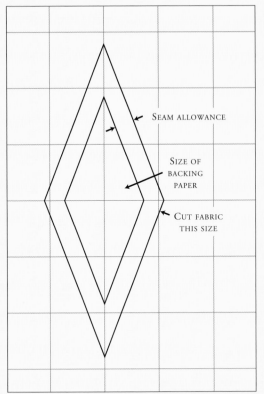

SEAM ALLOWANCE

SIZE OF BACKING PAPER

CUT FABRIC THIS SIZE

Patchwork – Saw-tooth Star Bag

CUT 1

CUT 4

CUT 4

GRAIN

CUT 8

Patchwork – Log-cabin Yarn Roll

LIGHTER FABRICS

DARKER FABRICS

Patchwork – Heart Cushion (Pillow)

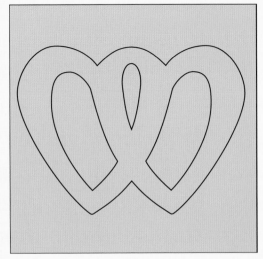

Appliqué – Star-fruit Panel

Appliqué – Cornucopia

Appliqué – Oven Glove (Mitt)

Appliqué – Goose Shopping Bag

Appliqué – Bolster Pillow

Appliqué – Apron

Knitting – Baby Wrap

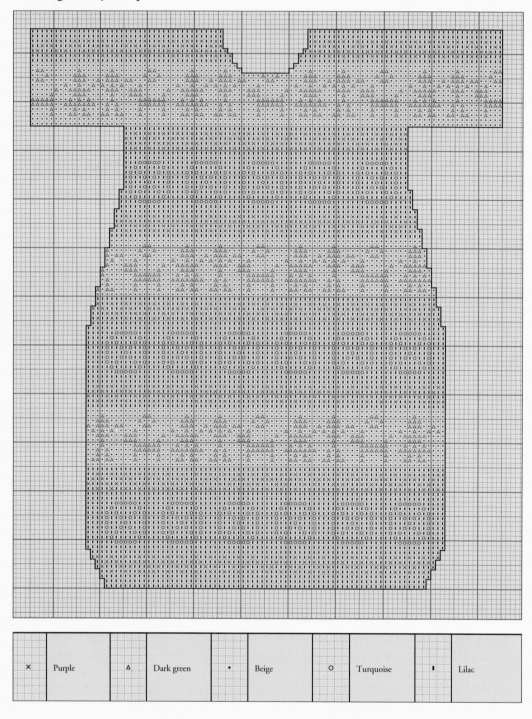

✕	Purple	▵	Dark green	•	Beige	○	Turquoise	ı	Lilac

Knitting – Ski Hat

•	Light grey	×	Dark green
○	Cream	□	Brown
△	Beige		

Knitting – Purse Bag

BUTTONS

Acknowledgments

CONTRIBUTORS

The author and publishers would like to thank the following textile artists
who designed and made the step-by-step projects:

Petra Boase Appliqué: oven glove (mitt), apron. Special techniques: fabric-strip rug.

Louise Brownlow Embroidery: fish mobile.

Sally Burton Embroidery: rag book.

Philippa Eccleston Appliqué: star-fruit panel.

Emma Ganderton Embroidery: potpourri bag. Needlepoint: cup and saucer. Quilting: linen throw.

Mary Ganderton Crochet: baby blanket and woollen balls, cotton duffle bag, coasters and placemat, curtain heading, jug (pitcher) cover, snowflake motif. Knitting: basket edging.

Angela Hauch Knitting: baby wrap, cable cushion (pillow), purse bag, ski hat.

Julie Johnson Knitting: baby mittens, baby shoes, tasselled hat, baby doll. Special techniques: pompom necklace.

Rachel Marshall Crochet: flower box, strawberry and tomato hats. Embroidery: folk art gloves.

Amy Poulton Knitting: Shetland lace scarf.

Isabel Stanley Embroidery: rocket bag, placemat, table cloth, picture frame. Needlepoint: jewellery box, circular star. Appliqué: bolster cushion (pillow), notice board. Special techniques: button mirror.

Amy Taylor Machine embroidery: cat picture.

Carole Tompkins Needlepoint: needlebook and scissor case.

Kelie-Marie Townsend Embroidery: house and garden picture, tea towel.

Karen Triffet Embroidery: hairslide (barrette), drawstring bag, hat.

Dorothy Wood Special techniques: sun dress.

Thanks to the following designers who allowed their work to be featured:
Andrew Bairstow, Louise Brownlow, Sally Burton, Karen Colley, Philippa Ecclestone, Andrew Timms, Carole Tompkins, Kelie-Marie Townsend, Sian Pile, Sarah Rubie, Anu Pama Yadav.

All other projects, techniques and examples designed and made by the author.

Special thanks also to: Hugh Ehrman, Louise Irvine of the Shetland Knitwear Associates, Alec and Jenny Hutchison at Strawberry Fayre, Cara Ackerman at DMC and Christine Kingdom from Offray for their help and enthusiasm; Carole Tompkins for her advice and encouragement; Belinda for her backing and perseverance; James, Madeleine and Elsa for their friendship and the photography; my parents Mary and Colin and my sister Emma for their unfailing and invaluable support, and to Jonathan for being there.

Suppliers

UNITED KINGDOM
Thanks to the following UK suppliers who so
generously provided materials:

Appleton Brothers Ltd
(Tapestry and crewel yarns)
Thames Works, Church Street,
London W4 2PE
020 8994 0711

The Craft Collection
(Paterna Persian yarn)
Terry Mills, Westfield Road, Horbury,
Wakefield,
West Yorkshire WF4 6HD
01924 810812

DMC Creative World
(Machine/hand embroidery threads, fabrics
and canvas)
Pullman Road, Wigston,
Leicestershire LE18 2DY
0116 2811040

Framecraft
(Frames and powder bowl)
372-376 Summer Lane,
Hockley,
Birmingham B19 3QA
0121 212 0551

Freudenberg Nonwovens LP
(Quilting, fusible bonding, and interfacing)
Vilene Retail, PO Box 3, Greetland,
Halifax HX4 8NJ
01422 313140

Redburn Crafts & Needlecraft Centre
Squire's Garden Centre, Halliford Road,
Upper Halliford, Shepperton,
Middx TW17 8RU
01932 788052

Shaker
(American homespun cloth)
25 Harcourt Street,
London W1H 1DT
020 7724 7672

Strawberry Fayre Fabrics
(Patchwork fabrics)
Chagford,
Devon TQ13 8EN
01647 433250

Telfords
(Card blanks and beads)
14 The Grove, Palmers Green,
London N13 5LG
020 8882 7729

CM Offray and Son Ltd
(Ribbon)
Fir Tree Place, Church Road, Ashford,
Middx TW15 2PH
01784 247281

US AND CANADA

Aardvark Adventures
(Cross stitch and embroidery fabrics, threads,
trims)
PO Box 2449, Livermore,
CA 94551
(800) 388-2687

Heartland Crafts Discounters
(Threads, yarns, tools)
Rte 6E, PO Box 65, Geneseo,
IL 61254
(309) 944-6411

Herrschers
(General needlecraft tools and materials)
Hoover Road, Stevens Point,
WI 54481
(800) 441-0838

Nancy's Notions
(Sewing, quilting, beadwork, appliqué,
embroidery)
PO Box 683, Dept 32, Beaver Dam,
WI 53916
(414) 887-0391

Yarnworks
(Knitting, crochet, cross stitch, dyeing)
519 Main Street, Grand Junction,
CO 81501
(303) 243-5365

Bettekaril's Needlecrafts
(Cross stitch, crochet, knitting)
PO Box 5008, Brandon,
MS 39047
(601) 992-3266

AUSTRALIA AND NEW ZEALAND

Coats Patons Crafts Pty Ltd
89-91 Peters Avenue, Mulgrave,
Vic 3170
1800 801 195

DMC Needlecraft Pty Ltd
51-55 Carrington Road, Marrickville,
NSW 2204
(02) 559 3088

Craft Ideas
Shop 2065,
Westfield Shopping Town, Indooroopilly,
Qld 4068
(07) 3378 4288

Bargello
819 Glenferrie Road, Hawthorn,
Vic 3122
(03) 9818 4853

Lazy Daisy
142 Burgundy St, Heidelberg,
Vic 3084
(03) 9457 2322

Needlecraft Mail Box
154 Mann Street, Gosford,
NSW 2250
1800 02 4942

Simply Stitches
153 Victoria Ave, Chatswood,
NSW 2067
(02) 412 4342

Glossary

AIDA CLOTH A double thread evenweave fabric, available in different sizes, which is used for cross stitch and counted thread stitches.

ANTI-FRAYING SOLUTION A proprietary liquid, available from department stores and haberdashers, which is applied to fabric to prevent cut edges from unravelling.

APPLIQUÉ An ornamental sewing technique, in which cut-out pieces of one fabric are sewn on to a contrasting background to form a design.

BASTING (SEE TACKING)

BATIK A resist method of patterning fabric, in which the areas not being dyed are covered with wax.

BATTING (SEE WADDING)

BEESWAX A solid block of natural beeswax is used to strengthen sewing or quilting thread and to prevent it fraying during work.

BIAS BINDING A strip of material cut on the bias, or cross grain, which is used to bind hems or for decoration.

BLOCKING Diagonally worked needlepoint stitches tend to distort the canvas, so the finished piece has to be damp stretched, or blocked, to restore the original shape.

BOBBIN The spool which holds the lower thread on a sewing machine. The tension can be altered by adjusting the screw on the bobbin case.

BOLSTER A long, cylindrical pillow or cushion.

BROCADE A rich, woven furnishing fabric with a raised design.

BRODERIE ANGLAISE A white cotton lace with machine embroidered decoration.

BUTT To join two ends together without overlapping them.

CALICO A white or unbleached coarse cotton fabric.

CHAMBRAY A woven cotton fabric with a white weft and a coloured warp, often used to make shirts.

CHECKERBOARD A pattern made up of alternate light and dark squares, resembling a chess board.

CHENILLE A textured, velvet-like yarn, originally used for embroidery, but now usually knitted. A chenille needle is thick, with a large eye and a sharp point.

COTTON LAWN A fine dress-making weight pure cotton fabric, often printed with floral patterns.

CREWEL Crewel work is a form of embroidery worked in a fine 2-ply wool (crewel wool) on linen, which was popular in the seventeenth century. The designs were based on natural imagery of plants, fruit and flowers. A crewel needle is sharp, with a long, easily threaded eye.

DÉCOUPAGE A method of decorating objects by sticking down cut-out shapes or pictorial motifs.

DENIM A hard-wearing twill (drill) cotton fabric.

DOUBLE KNITTING YARN A 4-ply wool, also known as knitting worsted.

DRESSMAKER'S CHALK Traditional tailor's chalk, in block or pencil form, is used to transfer designs or pattern marking to fabric. The marks can easily be brushed away.

DRESSMAKER'S FADING PEN Also called a quilting pen, this special felt-tip is used to draw designs directly on to fabric. Any marks made will fade completely within a few days. Water-erasable versions are also available.

EMBROIDERY HOOP A hoop, or tambour frame, consists of two wooden rings between which a piece of fabric is stretched, to produce a taut surface for embroidery.

FEED DOG The part of a sewing machine that feeds the fabric under the needle and presser foot to ensure a regular stitch. It is lowered for free machine embroidery.

FAIR ISLE A multicoloured style of knitting which originated in the Shetland Isles and which consists of intricate horizontal bands of pattern.

FOUR-SQUARE BLOCK Many traditional patchwork patterns are based on the subdivision of a square made up of four rows of four smaller squares.

FREEHAND STITCHING Machine or hand embroidery which is worked freely across the fabric surface, rather than over a given outline.

GAUGE (SEE TENSION)

GINGHAM A two-coloured woven checked fabric.

GROSGRAIN A heavy silk or rayon ribbon, woven with a textured rib.

GUIPURE LACE A machine-made lace in which the individual pattern motifs are joined by threads, rather than woven into a supporting net.

HABUTAI SILK A fine Chinese silk, available in many colours, often used for lining.

HANK A loop or skein of yarn or thread.

IKAT FABRIC A woven fabric on which the pattern has been formed by dying particular areas of the warp threads.

IMAGE TRANSFER SOLUTION A proprietary liquid, which is used to transfer a printed image from paper to fabric.

INDELIBLE FELT-TIP PEN A permanent marker pen, used for marking designs when the backing fabric will be covered completely with stitches, e.g. for tracing needlepoint designs on to canvas.

INTARSIA A knitting technique in which a multicoloured motif is worked on a plain background, also known as Jacquard.

IRON-ON FUSIBLE BONDING A paper-backed adhesive web, which is used for bonding two layers of fabric.

IRON-ON WADDING (BATTING) A bonded polyester fibre, with heat-activated adhesive on one side, used mainly for quilting.

ISOMETRIC GRAPH PAPER A type of graph paper used by architects, which is based on a grid made up of equilateral triangles, rather than squares.

LAMETTA Metallic foil strings or strips used for Christmas and other decorations.

LANOLIN The natural protective waterproofing found in sheep's wool.

LUREX The trade name for a fine glittering, metallic thread, or any fabric woven or knitted from the thread.

MITRE The method of finishing corners without overlapping the fold or seam.

MOIRÉ TAFFETA A watermarked woven silk.

MOTIF A design element which is repeated to form a pattern, or used singly.

MOUNTING BOARD (MAT) A versatile, medium-weight card-board, available in many colours, used in picture framing.

ORGANZA (ORGANDY) A fine, crisp fabric woven from silk or man-made fibres.

PERCALE A closely woven cotton fabric, which is often used for bed linen.

PERLÉ COTTON A lustrous twisted thread, available in several thicknesses, which is used for embroidery and crochet.

PERSIAN WOOL A woollen yarn, consisting of three separable strands, used for embroidery and needlepoint.

QUILTER'S SQUARE A clear plastic square marked with regular lines, used to measure and cut precise square pieces for patchwork.

RAFFIA A natural plant fibre derived from a species of palm. Artificial, brightly coloured versions are available from craft shops.

RICKRACK, BRAID A decorative zigzag woven braid used for trimming.

ROCAILLE BEADS Tiny glass seed beads, available in many colours, which are sewn down with a fine needle.

STRANDED EMBROIDERY THREAD A soft, loosely woven thread, which comes in six strands and which can be separated.

TACKING A large, temporary running stitch which is used to hold fabrics together before quilting or seaming, usually worked in a contrasting thread. This is taken out after the permanent stitches have been worked.

TAPESTRY FRAME An adjustable embroidery frame for supporting larger pieces of canvas or backing fabric.

TAPESTRY WOOL A twisted yarn used for working needlepoint.

TEMPLATE A pattern outline.

TENSION The number of stitches and rows to be worked per inch so that a finished knitted garment is the correct size.

TRAMÉ Laid threads worked on a double tapestry canvas.

TROMPE-L'OEIL A realistic image which has been designed to "deceive the eye".

WADDING A washable, polyester fibre, available by length, which is used as the padded filling layer in a quilt.

WARP THREAD The threads which run along the length of a woven fabric.

WATER-SOLUBLE FABRIC A plant-derived supporting fabric, used for machine embroidery, which dissolves in water.

WEAVER'S KNOT Also known as a reef knot, a strong flat knot used for joining two ends of thread.

WEFT THREAD The threads which run across the width of a woven fabric, from edge to edge.

Index

A

Afghan (grannie) squares	202
Aida cloth	36
Algerian eye stitch	21, 74
Alphabet sampler	34
APPLIQUÉ	122-153
Apron	146-147
Arrowhead stitch	17
Assisi work	20

B

Baby blanket	210
Baby doll	188-189
Baby mittens	180
Baby shoes	181
Baby wrap	178-179
Backing paper	95
Back stitch	16
Basket edging	175
Basketweave	169
Basketweave stitch	67
Beads	234-235
Bear's paw	97
Beeswax	95, 109
Blackwork	21
Blanket stitch	22
Blocking	66, 204
Bolster pillow	152-153
Bows	230
Braided rugs	226
Brighton stitch	71
Broderie anglaise	24
Broderie perse	130
Brooch cushion (pillow)	84
Bullion knot	23
Bullion stitch	45
Buttonhole loop	40
Buttons	236-237

C

Cable cushion (pillow)	174
Cable stitch	228
Cathedral window motif	103
Cat picture	51
Chain stitch	22, 196
Chair seat	118-119
"Charm" prints	38
Charts, making	64
Checked cushion (pillow)	108
Chenille yarn	186
Chequer stitch	71
Chevron stitch	17, 75
Circular needles	185
Circular star	81
Closed herringbone stitch	18
Close satin stitch	56
Coasters	216
Cold-water-soluble fabric	32
Colour, working with	65, 172-173, 197
Continental stitch	67
Coral stitch	23
Corded clusters	25
Cord quilting	107
Cornucopia	139
Couching techniques	27-47, 48
Craft paint	54
Crazy patchwork	100

Crazy quilt	114
CROCHET	190-221
Crossed stitches	72-73
Cross stitch	18-19, 72
Cross stitch charts	15
Cross stitch motifs	36-37
Curtain heading	218-219
Cushion (pillow) stitch	70

D

Detached chain stitch	45
Diagonal stitch	68-69, 78, 79
Domestic linen	116
Double couching	26
Double crochet	198
Double cross stitch	19
Double feather stitch	22
Double herringbone stitch	18
Double moss stitch	168
Double straight cross stitch	73
Double treble	199
Drawing on to canvas	64
Drawstring bag	47
Dresden plate	99
Dressmakers' carbon paper	15
Dressmakers' chalk	15
Dressmakers' pen	15
Dyeing	224-225

E

Edge stitch	48
Embossed ladder pattern	169
EMBROIDERY	8-57
Ermine filling	19
Even stitch tension	14, 31

F

Fabric bag	208-209
Fabric book	38-39
Fabric paint	41
Fabric-strip rugs	226-227
Fair Isle sweater	165, 173, 175
Feather stitch	22
Felt appliqué	134
Fern stitch	17
Filet crochet	204
Fisherman's sweater patterns	169
Fish mobile	54
Fishscale stitch	21
Florentine stitch	75
Flower box	206-207
Folk art gloves	44
Free stitch	28, 31, 50
Free straight stitch	31, 52
Free zigzag stitch	30
French knot	23
French seam	85
Fringed scarf	184
Fusible bonding	132

G

Garter stitch	162
Gathering thread	46
Gobelin filling stitch	75
Grid stitch	21
Guernsey sweaters	174
Guipure lace	131

H

Hairslide (barrette)	46
Half cross stitch	67
Half treble	199
Hand and machine quilting	104-105
Hand piecing	95
Hand quilting	104
Hawaiian quilt	136
Heart cushion (pillow)	120
Heart motif	80
Heraldic dragon	20
Herringbone stitch	18, 72
Hexagonal patchwork	98
Hexagon pincushion	121
Holbein stitch	20
Honeycomb darning	25
Honeycomb stitch	228
Horizontal stripes	197
Hot-water-soluble fabric	32
Hungarian diamond stitch	75

I

Image transfer	108
Intarsia	173
Interlaced double running stitch	48
Irregular running stitch	17
Isometric graph paper	121

J

Jewellery box	76
Jug (pitcher) cover	220

K

Knit and purl	162-163
Knit stitch	162
KNITTING	154-189
Knitting gallery	165
Knitted pattern stitches	168-169
Knotted stitch	16

L

Lace appliqué	131
Laced herringbone stitch	18
Ladder stitch	25
Lattice stitch	21
Lattice work	26
Lavender sachet	19
Lazy daisy stitch	22
Linen throw	116-117
Log-cabin yarn roll	112-113
Lone-star cushion (pillow)	78
Longarm cross stitch	18, 72
Looped and knotted stitches	22-23

M

Machine embroidery	28-29
Machine lace	32-33
water soluble method	32
Machine piecing	94
Machine quilting	105
Machine satin stitch	28
Mitring	52
Mola cloth	137
Mosaic cushion (pillow)	142
Moss stitch	168
Mountmellick work	24
Multi-directional satin stitch	28

KNITTING NEEDLES

US	METRIC	UK
0	2mm	14
1	2.25mm	13
	2.50mm	
2	2.75mm	12
	3mm	
3	3.50mm	10
4	3.25mm	
5	3.75mm	9
6	4mm	8
7	4.50mm	7
8	5mm	6
9	5.50mm	5
10	6mm	4
10.50	6.50mm	3
	7mm	2
	7.50mm	1
11	8mm	0
13	9mm	00
15	10mm	000

CROCHET HOOKS

US	METRIC	UK
14 steel	.60mm	14
12 steel	.75mm	
10 steel	1.00mm	
6 steel	1.50mm	
5 steel	1.75mm	
B/1	2.00mm	14
C/2	2.50mm	12
D/3	3.00mm	10
E/4	3.50mm	9
F/5	4.00mm	8
G/6	4.50mm	7
H/8	5.00mm	6
I/9	5.50mm	5
J/10	6.00mm	4
	6.50mm	3
K/10.50	7.00mm	2

N
Needle book and scissor case — **86-87**
NEEDLEPOINT — **58-87**
Nightdress case — **148**
Nine-star cushion (pillow) — **79**
Norwegian hardanger stitchery — **24**
Notice (bulletin) board — **149**

O
Oblong stitch variation — **73**
Openwork motif — **56**
Outline stitching — **106**
Oven glove (mitt) — **144-145**
Oxford frame — **82**

P
Padded appliqué — **150**
Padded quilting — **107**
Painted backgrounds, working on — **30**
Painting on to canvas — **64**
Paper, working with — **31**
Passementerie — **232**
PATCHWORK AND QUILTING — **88-121**
Patchwork gallery — **99**
Pattern cut appliqué — **136**
Perlé thread — **40**
Picture frame — **52**
Pinwheel stitch — **21**
Placemat — **50, 217**
Plain couching — **26**
Points and angles — **129**
Potpourri bag — **35**
Printed fabric appliqué — **130**
Pulled and drawn thread work — **25**
Purl stitch — **163**
Purse bag — **186-187**

Q
Quilting gallery — **106**
Quilting on patchwork — **105**
Quilting, three-dimensional — **107**

R
Ray stitch — **74**
Reverse felt appliqué — **135**
Reverse machine appliqué — **133**
Reverse stocking stitch — **163**
Rhodes stitch — **74**
Ribbon roses — **230**
Ribbons and bows — **230-231**
Rice stitch — **73**
Ridged bands — **168**
Rocaille beads — **234**
Rocket bag — **40**
Rosettes — **230**
Rotary cutter — **94**
Round, working in the — **101, 200**
Running stitch — **15, 16, 20, 40, 41, 42, 45**

S
San blas appliqué — **137**
Satin stitch — **16, 24, 40, 41, 45, 50, 51**
Saw-tooth star bag — **110-111**
Scottish Ayrshire work — **24**
Scottish stitch — **70**
Seed stitch — **16**
Shells and clusters — **203**
Shoe bag — **143**
Shoofly stitch — **21**
Single faggot stitch — **25**
Ski hat — **185**
Slip stitch — **198**

Small cushion (pillow) stitch — **70**
Smocking — **228-229**
Snowflake motif — **221**
Somerset patchwork — **101**
Space-dyed yarns — **224**
SPECIAL TECHNIQUES — **222-237**
Spiral couching — **26**
Square stitches — **21, 70-71**
Square weave — **35**
Star-fruit panel — **138**
Star stitches — **74**
Stem stitch — **16, 24, 45**
Stocking stitch — **163**
Straight stitches — **16-17, 75**
Strawberry and tomato hats — **212-213**
Strawberry motif — **15**
Suffolk puffs (yo-yo patchwork) — **102**
Sunburst cushion (pillow) — **133**
Sunflower motif — **201**
Sun pincushion — **83**

T
Table cloth — **56**
Tapestry frame — **14**
Tartan throw — **150-151**
Tasselled hat — **182-183**
Tassels — **232-233**
Tea towel — **41**
"Ten" stitch — **175**
Tent stitch — **67**
Threaded chain stitch — **22**
Three by three rib — **168**
Tied quilting — **118**
Tissue tacking (basting) — **15**
Top stitch — **47**
Trammed tent stitch — **67**
Transfer pencil — **15**
Transferring and charting (embroidery) — **15**
Transfers — **105**
Trapunto quilting — **107**
Treble — **199**
Treble circles — **200**
Trompe-l'oeil — **50, 149**
Two-part hoop frame — **14**

U
Upright gobelin stitch — **75**
Utilitarian denim — **40**

V
Vanishing muslin — **32**

W
Wave stitch — **169**
Whip stitch — **16**
Whipped running stitch — **47**
Whitework — **24**
Wire-edged ribbons — **230**
Woollen balls — **211**
Woven paper with ribbons — **31**
Woven stitch — **71**

Z
Zigzag stitch — **21, 169**

NOTES

NOTES

NOTES

NOTES

NOTES

NOTES

Notes

NOTES